RAM
THE ABDUCTION OF SITA INTO DARKNESS

Yael Farber

RAM
THE ABDUCTION OF SITA INTO DARKNESS

OBERON BOOKS
LONDON

First published in 2011 by Oberon Books Ltd
521 Caledonian Road, London N7 9RH
Tel: +44 (0) 20 7607 3637 / Fax: +44 (0) 20 7607 3629
e-mail: info@oberonbooks.com
www.oberonbooks.com

A catalogue record for this book is available from the British
Library.

ISBN: 978-1-84002-988-8

Cover photograph by Vinna Laudico

ORIGINALLY COMMISSIONED BY

THE CULTURE PROJECT

Artistic Director, Allan Buchman

Special Thanks

This adaptation was inspired by *Ramesh Menon's* magnificent prose retelling of *The Ramayana*. My profound gratitude for his opening the gates to the rest of us.

R.K Narayan & Ranchor Prime's short prose versions were also helpful. My thanks goes to the above and any other writers who may have impacted upon me while creating this text.

The ending I have chosen for this version of *The Ramayana* is inspired by an ancient Southern Indian tale and is recounted by Ramesh Menon in the final pages of his *Ramayana* retelling.

Allan Buchman – for choosing me to adapt this wonder.

Lekha Singh – for initiating & enabling this adventure.

Anant Jesse – for a rainy afternoon of black chocolate, orange juice and rama revelations in the garden.

Brian Drader – for your continued generosity, insights and exquisite gift for the lazer-precise questions that lead a writer to their own answers.

RAM

The abduction of Sita into darkness

"In the summer of 1988, sanitation workers across North India went on strike.[1]

Their demand was simple: They wanted the federal government to sponsor more episodes of a television serial based on the Indian epic Ramayana. The serial, which had been running on India's state-owned television channel for more than a year, had proved to be an extraordinarily popular phenomenon, with more than eighty million Indians tuning in to every weekly episode. Streets in all towns and cities emptied on Sunday mornings as the serial went on the air. In villages with no electricity, people usually gathered around a rented TV set powered by a car battery. Many bathed ritually and garlanded their television sets before settling down to watch Rama, the embodiment of righteousness, triumph over adversity. When the government, faced with rising garbage mounds and a growing risk of epidemics, finally relented and commissioned more episodes of The Ramayana, not just the sanitation workers but millions of Indians celebrated."

1 Pankaj Mishra in his Introduction to R.K Narayan's *The Ramayana*

Characters

VALMIKI SAMAJ[2]
Sanitation Workers, Keepers of the Sita-Body

RAMA
Ordained King of Ayodhya

SITA
Beloved of Rama

SITA - BODY
Body of Sita

LAKSHMANA
Brother of Rama

DASARATHA
Father of Rama

RAVANA
King of Sri Lanka

KAUSALYA
Mother of Rama

MANDODARI
Wife of Ravana

2 The word "bhangi" (sweeper) denotes an Indian caste. "Bhangis" are
treated as "untouchables" and typically belong to the "Valmiki Samaj" (a
sanskritised and perhaps more sanitized name than "bhangi"). "Valmiki
Samaj" are traditionally restricted to the sanitation work of cleaning
latrines and handling dead bodies (both human and animal). There
are a number of disparate communities, tribals, and nomadic groups
from different parts of India, who call themselves 'valmikis', claiming
to be descendants of Maharishi Valmiki, the first known author of the
'Ramayana'. (Susan Abraham's "A Sanitation Worker's Mumbai Dreams")

INDRAJIT
Son of Ravana

VIBHEESHANA
Brother of Ravana

SUGRIVA
Monkey King

VALI
Brother to Sugriva

HANUMAN
Monkey God Devotee of Rama

KUSHA AND LAVA
Street Urchin Sons of Rama

+ varuna; goddess of the sea
Incarnated by performer of the SITA-BODY

+ jatavu; ancient eagle warrior
Incarnated and / vocalized by performer of DASARATHA

+ garuda: half man half bird
Incarnated and / vocalized by performer of DASARATHA

+ the golden deer
Incarnated and / vocalized by performer of RAVANA

+the valmiki samaj
The valmiki samaj may be performed (as described in this text)
by the performers of KAUSALYA and MANDODARI. As with
all the additional characters above, performers doubling on roles
is optional.

Mise-En-Scene

The ideal performance space for RAM is a high-ceilinged urban-industrial room of stark, worn beauty. Seating is steeply raked to look down on and "hold" the performance on three sides or in the round. (Proscenium arch with a raised stage would be anathema to this work). The high ceilinged walls are covered in plastic-wrapped scaffolding, as though undergoing construction. The movement of the plastic sheets from the "wind" of large industrial fans, creates an unsettling, haunting sound. Before entering the performance area the audience is invited to remove their shoes and place them in a pile. Strewn around the performance area are piles of debris and tethered plastic bags – a bleak yet ethereal landscape of urban waste. Centre of the performance area is a large, ungainly television (circa 1970s) powered by a car battery and garlanded with dead flowers. The television screen is filled with the "searching" pattern of snowy static: the void we recognize when a television is sitting between channels. Static sonics fill the auditorium with its soft but disturbing sound.

The snow pattern of the television is reflected on the back wall of the space – creating epic presence from the banal domestic. Placed before the old television is a stunningly worn, long sofa. Seated in this sofa, standing behind and around it – is the full company [with the exception of the SITA-BODY, hidden beneath the waste of the landscape].

Prologue

As lights fade, the cast slowly rise from the sofa and drift away. The television is unplugged from the car battery by the last remaining members of the company and removed. Finally it is only the VALMIKI SAMAJ who remain. They sift through the layers of tethered plastic bags and waste, with a singular and unhurried air. Finally VALMIKI SAMAJ signals to the other. At her feet, curled in a fetal position and wrapped in plastic, is the body of a woman. She is handsome, naked and dead. The VALMIKIS cover their mouths with fabric, tear the plastic open and unwrap the broken SITA-BODY. They sing softly of death.

A woman rises from where she was concealed beneath the SITA BODY. Life force separates from its physical form. She stands beside the dead SITA BODY, but remains invisible to the VALMIKI SAMAJ. She is SITA.

SITA:
> Do not grieve for me. I am glad to go.
> Freer than you are, still in the body of pain.
>
> *(Regarding the SITA-BODY.)*
>
> This Body made only for sorrow.
> Burn after reading – but first read it well.
> There on the skin, in the bones, beneath the feet worn for this life
> Trace the journeys and dreams it once lived.
>
> *(One of the VALMIKIS tending to the corpse, speaks quietly.)*

VALMIKI 1: She was born – like she died – in a furrow of earth.
> Janaka found her in a field early one dawn, at the head of his
> plough. A few hours old, almost dead from the cold – he lifted
> her into his arms, named the foundling Sita, took her home
> and raised her as his own. Sita… Bearer of Great Sorrows.
> Wife to Rama in this lifetime. Lying naked in the dark folds
> of the Great Mother's skirt at birth – and now in death too –
> waiting once again to be taken home.
>
> *(Singing, the VALMIKI SAMAJ unfold the SITA-BODY from its fetal position and uncover two newborn infants – blue and suckling at her cold breasts.)*

VALMIKI 2: At the close of her life – she used the last she had, to tear the sons of Rama from her body, into this broken world.

(The VALMI SAMAJ lift the newborn boys from the SITA BODY and move away to her left and right. The umbilical chords remain attached growing longer as the VALMIKI SAMAJ move.)

VALMIKI 1: At the world's edge, the boys grew like orphaned buds in the wild. They spoke only in song. They sang only the story of their birthright: The Ishvaku Legacy carved forever on the tongues of Sita and Rama's sons.

(The VALMIKIS cut the umbilical chords. The babies scream. Their cries show the years that lapse, becoming the beautiful and haunting song of two street urchins KUSA and LAVA: RAMA's lost sons. Theirs is an ancient, dissonant sound – filled with beauty and grief. SITA stands amidst the urban detritus, dust and fluttering plastic bags.)

SITA: But let us not speak yet of loss, my beloved.
Let us sing rather of the beginning... When you first travelled beyond Ayhoda's walls. I found you at dusk – washing blood from your hands in the river outside my city. We were – neither of us – yet 16 summers old.

1: Essence

I.

(RAMA is kneeling at the water, cleaning his hands. He looks up to find SITA watching him.)

RAMA: Blood.

> *(She just looks at him.)*

> It gets in the nails…
>
> *(He looks away.)*

SITA: Whose blood is it on your hands?

> *(RAMA looks at her sharply.)*

RAMA: Those with blood on theirs.

SITA: Did their deaths heal what they harmed?

RAMA: No. *(Jaw clenched.)* But they will not harm again.

SITA: Then why, my lord, are you so sad?

> *(RAMA is quiet, he looks up to search her face.)*

RAMA: Where I'm from, life grows steadily, inevitably as trees. No one dies in Ayhoda who is not yet old.

SITA: Peaceful Ayhoda is all you have known?

RAMA: *(Nodding.)* It is my first time beyond the gates. I have seen things since that cannot be put into words. Mothers, children – used and buried, though not yet dead. The ground was still moving when we found them. All we could do… *(He cannot go on.)*

SITA: *(Nodding.)* The work of Ravana of Lanka's legions.

RAMA: *(Grimly.)* Blood does not wash easily, but I am happy for these stains.
I feel – perhaps for the first time – awake.

SITA: *(Smiling gently.)* Or have you just fallen into the slumber of duality from which few of us ever wake?

(RAMA nods, understanding her. The VALMIKIS exhale. RAMA puts his head down, overcome with grief. He covers his face. SITA goes to him, takes his hands, washes them, kisses each finger and then gently kisses each eye – including the third.)

SITA: *(Indicating her city over her shoulder.)* In Mathila too, they believe the world ends at the city gate. It is my daily practice since I was a child – to rise before dawn, and crawl the tunnel I made under the wall. I wake in a fever every morning and must wander into the wild – to see the truth for myself.

RAMA: Out here alone? What does your father say?

SITA: He does not know.

(He looks at her for a long moment.)

RAMA: Who are you, soul?

SITA: *(Smiling.)* No one knows to whom I was borne.
But I am the foundling of Janaka of Mathila. They call me Sita in this lifetime, my Lord.

RAMA: Are you promised?

SITA: Only to the mortal man who can string Siva's bow. *(She laughs gently at the absurdity of this.)* And so I am promised to no one at all!

(She smiles. He does not.)

RAMA: Show me this bow.

II.

(VALMIKI 1 moves around the SITA-BODY, singing of marriage. She begins to paint the naked flesh with intricate henna markings. VALMIKI 2 wraps SITA in the sari of a bride.)

SITA: Let us not sing yet of loss. Let us sing of how you found me, as you have in every lifetime… And once again brought me home.

(RAMA lays himself over the SITA-BODY, now animated with life, and pulls it into the embrace of their first wedding night. SITA watches from nearby.)

VALMIKI 2: The opening to the female body is but a portal to the great mystery of entering this fires of this realm; A gateway only accessible through Her form. The inevitable longing to possess her, is dark ego rising. That first longing for what can never truly be owned… Is the start of the sacred fall.

(She turns the SITA-BODY over, wipes the blood from between her legs and resumes painting her body. VALMIKI 1 removes the fabric covering her face and assumes the role of KAUSALYA – RAMA's mother. She gathers the naked, sleeping RAMA in her arms like a child.)

KAUSALYA: Much is written of a mother's love. What more need be said of the 9 moons I carried the blue one in my waters, before he passed through the static and into this world?

Childless in middle age, my husband performed a yagna begging that one of his three wives be blessed with a son.

(Lights rise on DASARATHA, with arms outstretched. He lets handfuls of dry, dusty rice pour between his fingers and scatter, smoking on the floor.)

The Gods answered with not one son from us – but four.

(The pipes of the scaffolding drip and form pools. The scaffolding's plastic coverings tremor and billow.)

History tells that when I bore Rama late into the night – I made no sound for "there was no pain". But his story too, was written by men. Too well I recall the white heat, as my body tore open. A woman can smile as she is drowning, no? *(A shower of petals from the skies.)* The future of Yuvaraja passed between my legs, as Rama – Dasaratha's first and most beloved son – was born.

III.

(DASARATHA, a powerful and aging man, holds KAUSALYA in a sensuous embrace. Her long dark hair hangs over her naked back.)

DASARATHA: (Confiding in her.) They say I love him too much.

KAUSALYA: Loving a child is constant preparation in grief.

DASARATHA: Do I love our son too much? What do you say?

KAUSALYA: Everything is Brahman, my Lord. Love him more – love him less. Someday, he too will be gone. (To audience.) Many years ago – my hair was still black… And my opinion still asked for.

VALMIKI 2: Many years ago – our hair was once black… And our opinions still asked for.

(VALMIKI 2 holds KAUSALYA's hair at the roots and pulls her fingers through it leaving the hair streaked with white. DASARATHA disappears from behind her, leaving her alone. She slips her robe over her shoulders and covers herself.)

KAUSALYA: Younger wives must have their time. What losses can we speak of as our beauty fades? And each day makes us a little more invisible still.

(VALMIKI 2 continues pulling white through KAUSALYA's hair.)

When Rama returned with beautiful Sita, his bride – I found reason again to dress and face the world. But ask any first wife: The waiting never leaves your soul.

(SITA stands behind KAUSALYA, and brushes her long graying hair. SITA's own black hair is striking in contrast.)

SITA: Tomorrow: Mother to a King.

(She sees KAUSALYA's stunned face.)

You did not know?

KAUSALYA: *(Embarrassed.)* It is many years since Dasaratha took my counsel. *(Gathering herself.)* It is his Dharma. Rama now belongs to his people.

SITA: Everyday, he will be less mine. How will I bear it. Ma?

KAUSALYA: Men cannot know grief until it sits at their table. We smell its shadow as children. We know its depth in the long nights of giving birth. In the agony of those hours, we brush shoulders with what waits for us all. Men know loss as death on the battlefield. We hear its song at the turning of each new moon.

SITA: *(Eyes tearing.)* Perhaps I am yet a child but without Rama I know I would die. As a shadow cannot be without its substance – I would simply cease to be.

KAUSALYA: The surrendering is the free-falling that we master, my dear. A smiling baby plunges from our arms and does not shatter its spine.

SITA: *(Brushing tears away, smiling.)* Tell me again of when he was born.

KAUSALYA: *(Combing SITA's dark hair.)* Rama came to us as dark as the forest… blue black. Lakshmana-born to Dasaratha's second wife – was pale and haunting as the moon. Two halves of the same lunar light. As children, they would sit for weeks watching the monsoons together – Lakshmana at Rama's knee. It has always been Lakshmana's dharma to protect his brother. Better yet… for what is to come…

SITA: Ma, why do you speak of loss on the eve of Yuvaraja? Tomorrow Rama will be King.

KAUSALYA: I am old, Sita. The future shows itself to me around the edges of the nights. I feel a tide moving in… And our heart will surely be born away when it draws back at dawn.

IV.

(KAUSALYA is braiding SITA's hair as they talk. RAMA has been watching them for awhile since he entered the room. LAKSHMANA waits behind him. RAMA's mother sees him and rises. He prostrates himself at her feet.)

KAUSALYA: Rise – King of all Tomorrows.

(He stands and she takes his hands.)

You're trembling.

RAMA: *(Not looking her in the eye.)* I've come to say goodbye.

(RAMA does not look at SITA but keeps his gaze steadily on his mother, who is silent for awhile.)

Our father is indebted to our fourth mother from many years ago. Tonight she has asked that he give her what she demands.

KAUSALYA: *(Beginning to understand the gravity.)* Shantam Paapam! Evil be still!

SITA: *(Barely able to breathe.)* What does he owe her?

KAUSALYA: *(Nodding, unable to look up.)* His life.
(They all look to KAUSALYA who moves to the fire.)

When Rama's father met Kaiyiki, she fast became his favourite and traveled with him… even to the battlefields during times of war. One night, as he lay dying from his wounds – beyond a woman's strength – she gathered him up and walked out of the encampment with him in her girl arms. He promised her any two wishes for saving his life. I see tonight – on the eve of your coronation – she has come calling on his unbreakable word.

SITA: What has she asked?

RAMA: *(Unable to look at SITA.)*
I will leave Ayhoda, before dawn, for fourteen years exile in the wild.

(SITA is stunned. KAUSALYA nods slowly, horrified but in recognition of her earlier unease.) And in my absence, Dasaratha will crown her own born son, Yuvaraja, in my place.

KAUSALYA: *(Understanding all.)* At last – Mother to a King.

RAMA: I don't have much time. I must leave before the city wakes.

(SITA looks wildly to LAKSHMANA who stands silently nearby.)

SITA: And Dasaratha agreed to this?

(LAKSHMANA nods, jaw clenched. SITA is breathless.)

Without his son, Dasaratha will die. Why would he blindly do as Kaikiki's ambition demands?

KAUSALYA: *(Quietly, looking at RAMA and LAKSHMANA.)* Because, my dear, the men of the Ishvaku House will honour a promise above all else.

RAMA: Leaving is my Dharma. *(Straining against the emotion.)* I am blessed to follow where it leads me.

LAKSHMANA: *(Unable to contain his disgust and rage.)* A King surely thinks what is best for his people, and not what suits his favourite whore!

KAUSALYA: No more, Lakshmana! I love Rama as you do. But that "whore" is one of four mothers to you both.

LAKSHMANA: As God is my witness, someday I will repay her. And the world will forgive me my sin.

RAMA: Kaiyiki is but an instrument of dharma, brother.

LAKSHMANA: *(Eyes filling with tears of rage.)* Not my mother by blood but mother all the same… I have loved her since I was a boy. But I will never forgive her this, Rama.

RAMA: Brother, we have sat side by side at our master's feet and learned dharma…

LAKSHMANA: And I must honour mine: To protect you always and from all things. Even a mother.

RAMA: The soul's path is eternal. What is fourteen years in the wild?

LAKSHMANA: Listen to me Rama. No one, not the Devas nor Kings would stand against your becoming King today. By violence, if needs be.

RAMA: *(Taking him squarely by the shoulders, looking into his eyes.)* Think with your cool head - not the fire in your heart. The Ishvaku men do not break their word.

(Turning to KAUSALYA.) Give me your blessing, please. *(Straining.)* At least let me go in some peace.

(KAUSALYA looks at RAMA intensely for a long moment.)

KAUSALYA: *(Quietly but resolved.)* Narayana give me strength every moment of these fourteen years ahead. I will be waiting for you, Rama. Go now, with my prayers.

(He lays himself at her feet. She lays her hand on his head. RAMA rises and turns to LAKSHMANA.)

LAKSHMANA: Nothing you say will matter. I go where you go.

RAMA: *(Smiles.)* I know better than to try. Go. Gather what we need and no more.

(They embrace. LAKSHMANA goes to KAUSALYA for her blessing, embraces her tenderly and leaves to prepare. For the first time since he entered the room – RAMA turns to SITA, with his eyes cast down.)

RAMA: Will you wait for me, my love?

SITA: Will you look at me, my lord.

RAMA: *(Managing finally to bring his eyes to meet hers.)* Will you wait until I return?

(Her eyes blaze with quiet anger. He is stunned as he has never seen defiance in her before.)

Perhaps the dharma I learned in my father's house is different here in Ayhoda. I was taught that a wife's path is to share her husband's fate.If you must walk the Danaka Vana for 14 years – it will be with your wife at your side.

RAMA: Sita, don't be naive. You will die out there. It is no place for even the most savage of men.

SITA: *(Simply.)* I am your wife in this life, and all the lives that follow. My place is by your side.

(VALMIKI 2 cleans the SITA-BODY. She begins to sing an old song of love.)

RAMA: *(RAMA takes in the full measure of his wife and nods.)* Janaki – we will walk together into the great darkness. May God watch over us and someday bring us home.

(They turn to KAUSALYA. She marks a tilaka on their brows and ties a raksha of protection around their wrists.)

KAUSALYA: Go while I am still strong.

(RAMA and SITA turn to go. Once alone – KAUSALYA prostrates herself full length on the floor and weeps.)

VALMIKI 2: *(To Audience.)* Before day breaks, the three walk away from Ayhoda in silence: Lakshmana holds the lantern up ahead; Sita is at Rama's back; the horses that carry their few possessions will take them to the forest edge. And then they are on their own.

DASARATHA: *(Running after them, crying out with desperation.)* Rama, Rama…

(He falls to his knees and begins to weep blood from his eyes. KAUSALYA pulls him into her arms.)

(The twin boys cry out in their haunting song.)

VALMIKI 2: How beautiful are the gardens of Ayhoda. How gentle the music we did not know we heard, until it is gone. Our breath in the dark, damp cavern of the mouth quickens, as blood moves through a heart now exiled from all it has known.

V.

(They have been riding for hours.)

SITA: You spoke me through each town and village we passed.

RAMA: Now the lands Ikshvaku was given by his father in the krita yuga.

SITA: And with each step, Ayhoda behind us, fell backwards into our future dreams of longing for the past.

(RAMA turns his face to the North from where they have come.)

RAMA: When will I see you again, beloved land of my ancestors? seven years twice over I will be gone. An eternity for those we leave. But for the Devas, less than a single day.
God willing – some day I will come home.

(He lies face down and kisses the earth. LAKSHMANA and SITA do the same.)

SITA: We released the horses to ride, empty saddled, across these great lands.

RAMA: Ride friends – back to Ayhoda. With you, take our souls.

SITA: We looked out at the magnificent waters of the Ganga. We knew, as darkness fell – that when we crossed the dark waters of that goddess in the morning – it would be many years, if ever, that we would return home.

RAMA: *(To SITA.)* Soul of souls: Talk to us of the Ganga. I need her legend on my broken heart.

SITA: *(SITA speaks in a low voice, to the soporific swell and flow of the waters.)* In times we can no longer recall – except in flickering shadows before we sleep – Himavan, the Emperor of mountains had two daughters. Uma was one. And Ganga the other. They say Ganga fell to us from the stars. She who flows at our feet is not only a river. But a Goddess who flows through our world.

(KUSA and LAVA's singing begins to build as SITA's tale fades. The VALMIKIS rub the dead SITA-BODY with a fine oil.)

VALMIKI 1: How perfect are the city walls that once held us – before the fall. How soon we forget that the sand too has a voice; the trees command life on the sidewalks of every city; and that truly we all answer to the same name.

(A growing golden light.)

When dawn broke – the brothers prepared for the great crossing over.

(RAMA and LAKSHMANA rise and apply the sticky milk of the pipal tree into their long hair. They coil their tangled locks onto their heads and change their clothes to the humblest of men. The transformation is stunning. They step into the boat.)

SITA: *(As they move out onto Ganga's waters, SITA quietly prays.)* Devi, Queen of that great body we call the ocean: Grant that in fourteen years, we will cross your waters again to come home.

VALMIKI 2: But as they move out into the deep, something stirs beneath. Somewhere, a shadowed figure opens its eyes and shakes off sleep. Again and again, through the ages, the darkness must be born.

(The VALMIKIS stretch the SITA-BODY out along the floor and cast water over the silent corpse. VALMIKI 2 steps away from the body and peels off her cloth to reveal a stunningly beautiful woman approaching middle age. This is MANDODARI. The STREET BOYS cry out their wild, beautiful song.)

2: Fall

I.

(RAVANA rises from his bed and moves to a window. The ocean below swells and rages. Battle-scarred, lithe and terrifying – he is an extraordinary presence. Beautiful but inscrutable, his wife MANDODARI rises too and stands nearby, watching his back.)

MANDODARI: Is there something my husband needs?

RAVANA: I dreamt of my Death... And she was beautiful.
(He turns, staring darkly at her.)
A woman's damp sex over my eyes, an eagle's dense feather plunging to earth, sleeper on the timeless ocean, singing my name. And I wanted more...

MANDODARI: Come back to bed.

RAVANA: Yes. But not yours. Death dreams always make me hunger. And you alone will not suffice.

MANDODARI: *(Turning away.)* As you please.
(Gripping her long dark hair, he pulls her towards him and forces her slowly to her knees. She stares up at him, a mixture of loathing and desire.)

RAVANA: *(Smiling.)* And I do please you, yes?

MANDODARI: *(A whisper.)* Yes.

RAVANA: Why then, Queen of the Rakshasas... Why always the black light from your eyes?
(MANDODARI pulls away in disgust.)

MANDODARI: You smell of your harem. Every one of your whores comes with you to my bed. They are on my sheets even after you are gone.

RAVANA: *(Pulling her up towards him from her knees, he violently tears away her robes. Suddenly his ten heads blossom on his shoulders. It is an awesome sight.)* But I bring you great pleasure, yes?

MANDODARI: *(Despite herself.)* Yes.

RAVANA: *(In her ear.)* I still feel you as you closed on me for the first time as a child. How you drew my tide again and again. *(She cries out, overcome.)* I know the anatomy of your surrender. It will always be mine.

(Pushing her brutally from him to the floor, where she covers her face with shame.)

What I don't know…is when I will come for you again. Perhaps the next moon. Or the one after that. I cannot be precise.

MANDODARI: Don't go… *(MANDODARI holds onto him as he walks away.)* Please. Come every day. Bring your whores.

(He pulls her face to within inches from his own.)

RAVANA: Still Beautiful, Queen MANDODARI: My First. Older… but beautiful yet!

(He shakes her from him and leaves. She falls to the floor, weeping and feverish for him, furious with herself but helpless against the continued tide of her pain and lust after all these years. She composes herself to the empty room, rises and goes to the window, but buckles over and weeps again.)

VALMIKI 1: One should never discount the beauty of Darkness. Even the Deva women fall to their knees in its embrace. For there is nothing as confounding as the pull of the great shadow. Out of it we are borne both away and towards ourselves.

II.

(RAMA, SITA and LAKSHMANA enter the forest. The VALMIKIS clean the feet of the SITA-BODY as they sing softly of paths that must be walked.)

RAMA: Be calm. Danaka Vana will feed on whatever we feel.

(The performer who plays DASARATHA, with blood still covering his eyes, holds aloft a magnificent eagle who flies above them. LAKSHMANA raises his bow and aims at the bird, but RAMA touches his arm.)

This is his home brother. *We* are the intruders here.

(They move forward into the dense foliage. The eagle never leaves them, flying above. Suddenly they stop dead in their tracks. In the clearing ahead – the bodies of women and children hang from the trees. SITA gasps and turns away.)

LAKSHMANA: *(Bow raised, ready to attack.)* In God's name who did this?

JATAYU: *(The eagle suddenly settles on a branch nearby.)* We do not say his name.

SITA: Ravana of Lanka.

RAMA: We are Kshatriyas from the House of Ikshvaku. We would have come sooner...

(He cannot go on, overwhelmed by what they have seen.)

JATAYU: We know who you are – Princes of Ayhoda. And Sita: Daughter to the Great Mother. We have been waiting for you through countless cycles. Everything painful that has led you this way, was an instrument in the unfolding plan. May it be ever blessed.

RAMA: You know who I am?

JATAYU: We do, Rama of Ayhoda.
Do you?

(RAMA stares at him, searching his ancient face. JATAYU stares back for the longest time.)

LAKSHMANA: *(Still overwhelmed by the sight of the dead children and mothers.)* This Ravana will know our names.

SITA: He is an expression of what lives in us all.

LAKSHMANA: *(Disgusted.)* No one can say I have the murder of children in my soul, Janaki.

SITA: We don't know who we truly are, brother... until we survive that long night of the soul.

JATAYU: Child of the Dharma...

RAMA: Who are you, ancient one?

JATAYU: I am Jatayu. Your father sent me from where he cannot come.

(RAMA lays down his weapon, trembling with emotion. He gestures in deference to the great bird.)

RAMA: Mighty one.

JATAYU: Danaka Vana is a complex nest of shadows. I offer what protection I can.

(JATAYU glances at LAKSHMANA, who has not yet returned his arrow to its quiver.)

With my life – if you only ask.

(RAMA nods to LAKSHMANA, who – on RAMA's command – returns his arrow, and presses his hands together in deference to the bird.)

RAMA: And we, the sons of the Ishvaku Line, give our word : We will not rest until we have ripped the dark by its roots, from these sacred soils.

JATAYU: Even if it is in yourselves that you find it thrives?

RAMA: *(Unnerved but steadfast.)* Even so. We give our unbreakable word.

JATAYU: Follow closely. I will bring you to a clearing for the night.

SITA: *(With a last glance over their shoulders at the murdered women and children.)* We follow you, Ancient one – with new fear yet hope in our hearts.

III.

(We find MANDODARI where we left her – bent over, weeping. She slowly stands erect and, with great dignity, rearranges herself. She looks at us.)

MANDODARI: I cannot recall a time before I was his. A virgin child-bride when I first stood before him. His battle-scarred body was a map I could not follow. His dark, brutal hands calling me closer, closer still. In his harem-the most beautiful from all realms, joined in opening me – their long fingers reaching inside to steal my essence. An expert in tantra vidya – he searched relentlessly for every portal into what was not yet formed. I emerged from his harem though only days later – decades old. Insatiable to this day, he comes to me each dawn after dozens of women – wanting more, more, more.

In the hours between his visits – I am a child of water stranded on the mainland. What else have I been grown for? What am I if not his? I would rather he comes, bathed in the low tide pungent scent of other women than not come at all. We don't know the smell of the shadows – but that they compel us to sell ourselves again and again, just for one moment more.

(MANDODARI's long dark hair spreads like a web in RAVANA's fingers, as he draws her back helplessly into his embrace.)

(She whispers.) Forgive me.

RAVANA: Always. The tide of this body you inhabit, brought Indrajit to manifestation's shores. More than any – that boy has my proud, savage soul.

MANDODARI: But it is a girl child you still ache for. We have all failed you in this. Time and again we push out new life. But never yet the redemption of a baby girl: The tender antithesis to all your brutality in this world.

RAVANA: My queen knows me best. Sons – I have hundreds of… borne from these loins. *(He laughs with self-irony.)* Perhaps in preparation for the ongoing wars of my own soul.

(MANDODARI watches him carefully, inscrutably as he walks away.)

IV.

(RAMA's eyes search the dark – as the reality of the dangers around them becomes increasingly real. His despair is growing.)

RAMA: How did I let you leave with me?
This is my Dharma to endure alone.

(He covers his face with his hands. They both turn to him and touch him tenderly.)

SITA: Husband to me in this life, in all the lives that came before and those yet to come –

LAKSHMANA: I will find some fuel for the ring of fire we will need to keep the wild beasts away through the night.

(LAKSHMANA gathers wood and materials, and lights a ring of fire around the three of them. But SITA stands at the periphery of the fire. RAMA goes to her.)

RAMA: What is it, my love?

SITA: Dharma is a tender thing, my Lord.

RAMA: *(Gently.)* Go on.

SITA: I know you will protect me always. But promise me, Rama… Promise me you will never strike until struck. Dharma, my love, is peace – most of all.

RAMA: Janaki, those who dwell in the ashrams of this forest sitting tapasya, are the gatekeepers of the world. To protect them is the very reason fate has called me here.

SITA: My soul – I too am here for a reason: To watch over *your* dharma. I have known this since I first saw you at the river, washing blood from your hands as a boy. Your spirit is my charge. And always I will say to you: Life is sacred – even in the darkest of men.

RAMA: *(Taking her face in both his hands and looking her in the eyes.)* Janaki, every sorrow we have lived, is a dark thread leading to my true purpose here.

SITA: You know I do not frighten easily, Rama. But something wild has been awakened. It lurks around the corners of these, our bright days. And I feel more fear than I ever have in my life.

(LAKSHMANA appears again from the dark.)

LAKSHMANA: Forgive me for intruding. Something moves swiftly this way. I felt its pulse in the earth as I lay down. It will be here soon.

RAMA: Take Janaki to the cave we saw earlier and wait there with her, brother. I will do this alone.

SITA: Rama…

RAMA: This is what the Dharma brought me here for, soul. This is only the beginning.

(To LAKSHMANA.) Go.

(After a beat, SITA nods and allows LAKSHMANA to lead her away, leaving RAMA alone in the circle of fire. We feel the pulse as the threat moves across the forest towards him. With a bow in his quiver, he stands ready.)

V.

(RAVANA is eating with relish. His brother, VIBHEESHANA waits silently for his response to the news he has brought. MANDODARI stands nearby watching the exchange.)

RAVANA: How many?

VIBHEESHANA: Every one of our fourteen thousand is fallen, my Lord.

RAVANA: Gifted though they must be to have razed Khara's invincible army – they do not know Ravana of Lanka. They will pay a brutal price.

VIBHEESH: Not "they" my Lord – but "he."

(All ten heads rise and swivel to look at VIBHEESHANA. The effect is astounding. Though he is used to his brother, VIBHEESHANA shrinks in terror.)

One man, with bow and arrow alone, killed them all.

(The ten faces begin to hiss. It is a terrifying sound. Then each head begins to talk at once.)

RAMA: A mortal?

VIBHEESH: Rama of Ayhoda. His lineage is the noble race of Surya; From the Royal House of Ikshvaku.

(RAMA, inside the ring of fire, defends himself against the onslaught.)

We – the handful who survived – no longer sleep. The calm beauty of his face haunts me still.

(RAMA stops fighting and looks around at the ground strewn with corpses. Shimmering petals rain down on him as he stands perfectly still.)

(RAVANA moves to the window and stares out at the sea below.)

RAVANA: I do not usually extend this honour – but I will go to Janasthana to kill this "Blue Prince" myself.

VIBHEESH: Lord of all the Worlds, hear me: He shone like a God when he faced our army. Through it all – he barely took a breath.

RAVANA: Are you saying this mortal is beyond me, brother?

VIBHEESH: I am saying: This is a mortal... But no ordinary man.

(Suddenly and quietly, MANDODARI speaks.)

MANDODARI: Nothing is beyond you, Lord of all the worlds.

(They both turn, in astonishment, to listen to her. She has never spoken to RAVANA of matters beyond her limited role.)

RAVANA: *(Intrigued.)* Speak. You have my ear.

MANDOR: Rama has a wife – Sita. She who followed her husband into the forest when a lesser woman would have forsaken a man. Sita, whom Rama of Ayhoda loves more than his own life. They are one another's prana, Lord.

RAVANA: Go on...

MANDOR: The apsaras of Devaloka are no match for her beauty. Her face a work of art – her body a vision. We must have her Ravana. While that woman is in the world, there should be no peace until the most powerful being in this realm makes her his own.

VIBHEESH: *(With quiet outrage.)* Mandodari, there is no greater sin than to steal a man's wife.

MANDOR: *(Ignoring VIBHEESHANA, she continues.)* If you were to abduct the beautiful Sita – not only would the most exquisite woman in the three worlds complete our Harem... But Rama of Ayhoda would be conquered. His heart...

RAVANA: *(His dark eyes, glittering, fixed on MANDODARI.)* Cleft in two.

MANDOR: Rama has made the fatal error you never would. He truly loves a woman. No skill on the battlefield, no cunning or brute strength, can protect one from grief. Slow, unfolding grief that gently but inevitably kills.

(All ten of RAVANA's heads turn to look at her. They begin to smile. He pulls MANDODARI to him. VIBHEESHANA backs away and out, leaving them alone. RAVANA tears her clothes from her and repeats SITA's name, like a mantra, over and over again.)

VI.

(DASARATHA stands in a mule cart. He has a garland of wild flowers around his neck. He is slowly pulling the long white hair out his head. He tears his clothes away until he stands naked, old and frail in the wind.)

(SITA lies beside RAMA, turning in her sleep. We see that DASARATHA is the vision she dreams.)

(DASARATHA cups dark soil to his mouth and eats.)

(SITA starts awake. She cries out.)

RAMA: What is it, Sita?

SITA: *(Looking at RAMA and LAKSHMANA.)* Dasaratha.

LAKSHMANA: Sita, you were dreaming.

SITA: Sons of the Ikshvaku Line: Your Father is dead.

(RAMA walks away into the dark, knowing it is true. He falls to his knees. LAKSHMANA goes to RAMA.)

LAKSHMANA: Brother…

RAMA: There is no Ayhoda for me now.

LAKSHMANA: Your people wait for you Rama.

RAMA: What other man has lived that once held my small hand in his.

(He waits until RAMA's weeping subsides. He touches him gently.)

LAKSHMANA: Let us offer tarpana.

(RAMA looks at his brother. Slowly he nods, gathering himself. The VALMIKIS sway and hum an old song of despair. RAMA wades into the

river until he is waist deep. LAKSHMANA follows but stays at a distance in the water. SITA watches from the shore. RAMA faces south and raises his arms to the skies.)

RAMA: Father, you have been gathered back to the Father's in Pitriloka.

LAKSHMANA: Dasaratha of Ikshvaku: we eat this fruit in your name. Your sons thank you for the gift of life and swear to honour you to our last breath.

(The brothers eat the fruit. RAMA gives some to SITA. They rise and begin to walk. LAKSHMANA walks ahead.)

RAMA: Janaki, I am lost…

SITA: *(She takes his face in her hands.)*
But not alone. I walk beside you, Lord Rama.
In this life and those to come…
I am yours.
(She kisses his eyes, like she did when she met him as a boy.)
(The twin boys sing out as we see dawn break. RAMA and LAKSHMANA worship the new sun with Suryanamaskaru.)

SITA: Danaka Vana came to trust us, as we did it. Lakshmana built us a humble home in the deepest part of the wild. And one could say – without restraint – that we were happy. Were we not beloved? Were those not our sweetest years? Outside of our sanctuary, the genocide continued like a dark beast rolling downhill. You tried to protect me from what lay beyond the light. But I have always understood sorrow, my beloved. It was sorrow that led me under my father's city wall to find you as a girl. It is sorrow, after all, that drew me to the golden creature. Her sorrowful eyes looked into my soul.

I have been held much responsible for what happened next. And though they will say it is the woman's heart easily drawn to temptation… she sang to me of sorrow. And I answered her call. I would rather mistake evil for sorrow a million times over – than walk away in fear from something that cries out for help.

(RAVANA stands between shadows and shafts of light. LAVA and KUSA sing in low tones, as RAVANA opens his dark coat, releasing an exquisite, shimmering deer. SITA is stunned by its other-worldly beauty. It comes toward and nuzzles her. She is transfixed.)

SITA: Who are you, fine one? From what part of me?

(RAMA and LAKSHMANA come up behind her.)

RAMA: Whose work is this?

SITA: *(She moves again towards the creature and notices it is weeping silent tears.)* Why do you weep, child? What sorrows are yours?

LAKSHMANA: *(Backing away.)* No animal of this realm weeps. Brother, now is the time to be awake.

SITA: I am gifted to hear the voices of all creatures – but yours is silent to me. Why?

RAMA: *(Looking at SITA with the same love she looks with upon the deer.)*

(To LAKSHMANA.) Never have I known a person to encompass such compassion for all life.

LAKSHMANA: Brother wake up. You are both enchanted:

(The animal suddenly darts away from SITA into the thick of the forest.)

SITA: Rama – she is new born and not yet steady on her feet. The wild beasts will have her before night. Save her. I beg you, beloved.

LAKSHMANA: Brother, hear me! This is no earthly creature. Her beauty smells dark.

RAMA: If you are right – I will know it when I have her and I will kill her without a moment's pause. If she is who Sita believes her to be – a foundling needing protection like she once was – then Sita will have the only thing she has ever asked of me. Do not leave her for even a moment. I will be back soon with the golden creature – either dead in my arms or walking by my side.

SITA: Find her, Rama. Or we are lost.

(RAMA nods, and moves off swiftly into the thick of the forest. He turns back once, waves to SITA – and is gone.)

SITA: *(Becoming lucid, emerging from the trance.)* Brother, that creature conjured my own ancient grief. I recalled myself at both birth and death, in a furrow of earth, waiting to be found.

(LAKSHMANA is silent. His grave concern hangs in the air.)

SITA: Have I sent Rama to great danger?

LAKSHMANA: I believe you have, Sita... yes.

(RAMA pursues the golden deer. It is a complex and beautiful pursuit, as the shimmering creature moves between shafts of light in the the dark of the forest. RAMA raises his bow several times – but is moved to pity and lowers his weapon. Suddenly the creature stops and RAMA sees, in his mind's eye, SITA as she waved goodbye to him. In SITA's voice, the deer suddenly speaks a single, chilling line.)

SITA as DEER: The gate is open – and she is lost.

(RAMA's face is suddenly stricken with panic for, in an instant, he understands all.)

RAMA: NO! *(He shoots the deer through the heart, and cries out in warning.)* SITA! LAKSHMANA!!!

(He begins running back to their sanctuary, but dark has fallen and in his pursuit of the deer he had wandered further than he thought. He stumbles, groping blindly as the roots and branches of the trees reach out to restrain him. He fights ferociously, calling out.)

SITA! LAKSHMANA!

(They both turn in the direction of RAMA's cry.)

SITA: That was my Rama. Go to him, Lakshmana! Fly!

LAKSHMANA: I gave Rama my word I would not leave your side.

SITA: Go to him or he will die.

(A shadow crosses over her face. She steps back in horror.)

You want him dead to make me yours!

LAKSHMANA: Janaki, calm yourself...

SITA: *(Turning her burning eyes onto him.)* I have known it always.
I have seen you watching me… In the mornings at the river
when I wash. You have waited patiently for this day! You are a
blot on the Ikshvaku name!

(LAKSHMANA looks at her – devastated like a child.)

Somewhere in your soul's darkest reach – you want your
brother dead.

*(LAKSHMANA presses his hands over his eyes in agony at this decision.
Then he moves suddenly around SITA, and draws a circle of light.)*

LAKSHMANA: Stay within this circle. It will hold you until I
return. If you break beyond it, I cannot bring you back again
into light.

(Looking her in the eyes.)

May God forgive you Janaki.
May God forgive us both.

*(LAKSHMANA turns and disappears into the forest in the direction of
RAMA's voice.)*

*(SITA chants the Vedas softly to herself – trying to contain her panic.
She hears a deep sigh.)*

SITA: Who is there in the dark?

*(RAVANA steps out of the shadows. SITA steps back in fear. RAVANA is
searching her face – utterly transfixed.)*

RAVANA: I am lost.

SITA: *(Looking deeply into his eyes.)* Yes.

*(They stand like that for a long time. RAMA, in his battle with the forest,
calls out – but SITA can no longer hear him.)*

RAMA: *(Calling out desperately.)* Sita! SITA!

RAVANA: May I come nearer.

SITA: I am protected by the Rekha's circle of light.

(RAVANA falls to his knees. He is weeping. He covers his face in shame.)

Why do you weep?

RAVANA: In your eyes, I see myself as I am.

SITA: And who are you?

RAVANA: Ravana of Lanka.

(SITA steps back in naked terror, but the compassion does not leave her eyes.)

SITA: You have much to weep for, Ravana of Lanka. I have seen your work.

RAVANA: I am backwards standing before you. I am at the bottom of the ocean as you whisper to me, floating through currents of time. I want to weep and I know not why, but that you look at me as the man I was before Ravana of Lanka became my name. I want to lie at your feet and for you to find me another name.

SITA: Names are but shifting shadows.

RAVANA: Everything but my name is long dead.
(Proudly.) I am the Rakshasa that conquered the world.

SITA: And this brings you joy?

RAVANA: It brings me power.
You bring me home. Every man wants to be forgiven by she who sees him anew.

SITA: The essence remains, no matter how far we have wandered.

RAVANA: You are wrong, daughter. Some of us are lost, forever.

SITA: And in saying so – found again.

RAVANA: Let me take the dust from your feet.

SITA: It's not possible. The circle protects me.

RAVANA: If my essence of good remains, why then do you need protection?
(She hesitates.)

Beautiful words of faith… but hollow, my dear.
(She looks up sharply.)

Forgive me. I would not trust me either.

(He turns to go.)

SITA: I ...

RAVANA: For a short time while you looked at me – I remembered who I once was.

SITA: Come let me bless you, Ravana of Lanka. Let me offer faith where there has been none. You have destroyed countless lives in this realm but if I forgive you, then surely we all rise.

RAVANNA: You are trembling.

SITA: I am deeply afraid. But you are too.

(SITA steps out of the occult circle and it starts to fade.)

VALMIKI 2: *(Sighs.)* And so like a stone rolling downhill, destiny takes its course: The abduction into darkness of the self.

(LAKSHMANA and RAMA running wildly, collide. They grab each other and begin to wrestle ferociously. Realizing their error, they stop and look at each other.)

RAMA: *(Grabbing LAKSHMANA.)* Where is she? Brother, where is Janaki?

LAKSHMANA: She heard you cry out! She would not let me stay with her, but insisted I come to protect your life.

RAMA: I TOLD YOU NEVER TO LEAVE HER SIDE! O god! O dear god! Janaki...

(He runs back towards the sanctuary, calling her name. LAKSHMANA follows. They come to the fading, empty circle of light.)

RAMA: What have you done? *(Shaking his brother who is weeping like a child.)*

LAKSHMANA: Forgive me, brother. Forgive me...

(RAMA grabs LAKSHMANA in a fierce embrace as he weeps.)

RAMA: O god brother... What have we done?

(The STREET URCHINS – KUSA and LAVA – cry out, as lights fade.)

3. Monkey Mind

I.

(Lights grow on HANUMAN: A magnificent half monkey-half man. A soft piece of fabric from Sita's clothing floats down from above. He reaches out with one hand and effortlessly catches it. He looks up to where it came from.)

HANUMAN: She is beauty that can only be spoken of in the voices of the rain. Golden of skin, hair like seaweed from the deepest ocean-leagues below where no light is seen. Yet it is the compassion in her lotus eyes that sets her apart. Borne of the great mother herself, there can be no doubt.

(Lights grow further and we realize he is talking to SUGRIVA. A monkey-man like HANUMAN.)

SUGRIVA: Forget you ever saw her taken. She is a whisper in the halls of Lanka now.

HANUMAN: She is Sita. Wife to Rama of Ayhoda.

(SUGRIVA turns in astonishment to look at HANUMAN – then turns away, shaking his head.)

SUGRIVA: Ravana of Lanka has any woman he wants. Long ago he was cursed never to force himself on a woman again. And so he has learnt to garden subverted desire and rob the essence of even the strongest feminine soul. Forget Rama, Hanuman. His wife belongs to Ravana now.

HANUMAN: *(Daring himself to be frank.)* My Lord – you know what it is to lose everything! To be exiled from your mother land and have your woman taken into the night.

(SUGRIVA is silent. The mention of his own exile and lost wife have pierced him to the core. He waits for the pain to flow away. HANUMAN stands quietly – unsure how SUGRIVA will take his naming the unmentionable. Finally SUGRIVA speaks.)

SUGRIVA: Find Rama of Ayhoda and bring him to me.

(HANUMAN turns and is lifted into the arms of his father – the wind.)

II.

(RAMA and LAKSHMANA are moving through the forest, searching for SITA. RAMA is frantic with despair. We have never seen him like this.)

RAMA: *(To the trees. to the river.)* Have you seen her – ancient ones? Did you see where Sita went?

LAKSHMANA: Brother, no one saw her go.

RAMA: *(To the mountain, in rage.)* Tell me what you saw! You have been here since before time - but I swear, I will end you! I am Rama of Ayhoda... SPEAK!

(Stumbling to his knees, he holds his head in his hands. He begins to weep.)

LAKSHMANA: Rama, be calm. Nothing will come of losing yourself.

RAMA: *(To LAKSHMANA, with chilling resolve.)* From today I am another man! With my hands I will tear the earth down to its core. I will turn the sun to ash and silence the stars. Darkness will reign – until Sita is again by my side.

(RAMA draws an awesome shaft from his quiver, and begins fitting it to his bowstring. LAKSHMANA falls at his feet.)

LAKSHMANA: I beg you, Rama. This is not the way of the Dharma!

(A gust of wind blows a mass of feathers that fly about his feet. RAMA drops his bow and stumbles along a trail of blood. They find JATAYU dying nearby.)

RAMA: Noblest friend…

JATAYU: Lord Rama. Sita has been taken South.

RAMA: By whom, ancient warrior?

JATAYU: I swore to protect her. But I am old and he stormed the skies.

RAMA: Who took my Sita?

JATAYU: Hold me Rama. I am going into the great darkness now.

(RAMA takes the magnificent bird in his arms as he dies.)

LAKSHMANA: *(Looking at the silent and still RAMA with new awareness.)* Brother, for a moment – I was more afraid of you than anyone I have ever known. You are more than I ever guessed. More than I can know.

(RAMA says nothing. He stares fiercely into the gathering storm.)

III.

(SITA lies unconscious in a dank cell. RAVANA crawls towards her – serpentine – along the floor. Elevating himself on his arms above her. She shifts and he backs away suddenly into a corner. SITA wakes, looks around with growing fear and then finds RAVANA staring at her from the dark corner.)

RAVANA: My love…

SITA: *(With terrified, dawning comprehension that she has been abducted.)* No…no…where is Rama? What is this place?

RAVANA: You will love me, Sita…

SITA: Mother, mother, mama, ma…I cannot keep back this tide. I do not have the strength…

RAVANA: Let me be strong for us. I am fiercer than the mind can hold.

(But SITA is not talking to him. She seems to be communing – in her terror with another presence.)

SITA: This is the Lingam without Yoni. This is the power without its base; The force of the pull without the moon's balance. Great Mother, this is the Shiva-Linga that can no longer see itself.

RAVANA: I will lie and die in you. Push my way through.

SITA: Rama, find me! Or we are all lost.

(RAVANA moves towards her. SITA picks up a blade of grass and points it at him. RAVANA clutches at his groin and backs away. He begins to weep, with pain and desire, like a child.)

SITA: Mother, he cannot see the Yoni at the base. The sacred balance forever lost…

We will stumble in his questions for long ages. Darkness will spread until Shiva-Linga stands where Yoni can never resume her place.

(RAVANA holds himself, weeping. Finally he stands over her.)

RAVANA: I am the golden deer you sent Rama into the darkness to pursue. You brought this upon yourself. Now or later you will know the depth of your own desire. And when you do – you will never want to find your way home again.

(He turns and walks away from SITA who stares at the wall trying to contain her pure, naked terror.)

IV.

(RAMA and LAKSHMANA have been stumbling through the forest for days, searching for SITA. HANUMAN observes them for some time from a hiding place. RAMA kneels in the earth and begins to chant the Vedas through gritted teeth, but is soon overwhelmed.)

(The VALMIKIS watch impassively from the periphery.)

VALMIKI 2: Into the belly of the great Danaka Vana we must all drift alone. Our only means of navigation: the chattering monkeys of the mind! But amongst them lives devotion – waiting to be harnessed and quietly heard.

HANUMAN: *(Stepping out to reveal himself.)* Brothers, why have you come to this desolate place?

LAKSHMANA: *(On the defense, with bow raised.)* Who is asking?

(HANUMAN reaches out and offers RAMA the fabric from SITA's dress. RAMA stumbles back. LAKSHMANA slowly takes it from HANUMAN. Then instantly raising his bow again.)

This is Sita's. How do you come to have it?

HANUMAN: Some days ago – the sky was filled with her cries. I looked up to see a Rakshasa with a woman in his arms, struggling for her life. What she dropped, floated like a broken wing, into my open palm.

(RAMA holds the fabric, lost in the touch and scent of SITA.)

LAKSHMANA: Who are you? For whom do you speak?

HANUMAN: I am Hanuman – son of the Wind God Varayu. Sugriva sent me to find you.

LAKSHMANA: Sugriva, once King of the Vanaras?

HANUMAN: You have heard his story?

LAKSHMANA: I have heard that he is just and true.

HANUMAN: Driven from his Kingdom by his brother Vali, his wife and home stolen from him –

Sugriva lives as an outcast now – fearing everyday his brother will come for his life.

(RAMA is quiet for some time. He finally lifts his head and speaks.)

RAMA: If your King Sugriva and his Vanaras will help me find Sita – I will do the bloodletting he cannot.

LAKSHMANA: *(Taking RAMA aside.)* Rama, this trouble between brothers is none of our concern…Remember your promise to Sita, my Lord!

RAMA: Just as you knew you must follow me into the Wild…I know my Dharma is to walk where Hanuman leads me today.

(LAKSHMANA is silenced by this thought.)

(To HANUMAN.) Take me to Sugriva. He is my brother in grief.

VALMIKI 1: Monkey heart. Monkey mind. The carousel of endless possibilities turning in the vortex of longing. And then one sharp morning – devotion walks into our field, drops to the soil and begins planting new seeds.

(As the VALMIKIS turn the SITA-BODY over, they sing of HANUMAN's devotion, and sponge the lifeless SITA-BODY.)

V.

(RAMA and SUGRIVA fiercely embrace. LAKSHMANA and HANUMAN stand silently, watching over the lives they have each devoted themselves to. SITA, in her far off confinement, finds refuge in her vedas. Beneath her chanting, we hear SUGRIVA by the fire, telling RAMA his story.)

SUGRIVA: For many years there was great love between me and Vali – much like between you *(Referring to Lakshmana.)* and your blood here. Vali was older brother to me; But equally Father, Soul's Friend and Guru. I have loved him since before we were both conceived. When Vali grew to be King – I wanted only to serve him with my life. One night, an Asura challenged my brother over a woman. We of monkey mind, are ruled by the passions of our blood. To kill over a woman is, for us, not an uncommon thing. When the Asura saw me and Vali coming for him in the full moon's light – he fled into the forest and vanished into a cave. Vali told me to guard the entrance as he went in. I waited at the cave mouth for hours, which turned to days, then weeks and months! I ate only what the nearby trees offered. I hardly slept. But one night – after ninety-two moons, I heard Vali scream. A stream of blood – dark like a vanara's – flowed from the cave at my feet. I rolled a boulder over the entrance and ran for my life. Back in Kishkinda, I offered tarpana to my dead brother's spirit and, still grieving, was crowned by Vali's ministers who thought he would never return.

One morning months later, I woke to find Vali standing over my bed. He was exhausted but alive. I wept for joy. But he stripped the blankets from me and looked only at the the golden rings on my toes, and the crown beside my bed. "Murderer" he whispered with burning eyes, and chased me through the three worlds. This mountain is the one place Vali is cursed not to set foot. And so I hide here. He lives as King now. He sleeps between my wife's legs, with my homeland and future in his hands. If I leave the sanctity of this mountain, he will hunt me down and make me pay for a kingdom I never stole… but one which was given to me by those who thought he would never return.

(SUGRIVA is weeping. RAMA holds him in an embrace again.)

RAMA: Take me to your brother, Vali. It's time to go home.

(A memory of SITA appears at RAMA's right shoulder.)

SITA: Promise me, my love! Promise me.
Dharma is peace – most of all.

RAMA: *(Looking over his shoulder.)* Sita?

(But he is alone.)

(KUSA and LAVA sing in their dissonant tones, as SITA – in her cell – reaches towards the moonlight streaming in from a small window.)

VI.

(SUGRIVA stands opposite VALI. They face each other, locked in a mutual stare. A deep rumbling growl emanates from them both. The effect is awesome and ominous.)

VALI: Have you grown so tired of exile that you prefer to die?

SUGRIVA: When will you know it was your own ministers who crowned me.

VALI: If you come seeking forgiveness – leave now with your life.

SUGRIVA: I am ready to die or kill you… rather than live this exile another day.

(VALI roars with laughter.)

VALI: You are powerful, Sugriva – but you do not have my stamina. You will grow tired and stumble under one of my blows. But unlike when we were children – I will not lift you from the earth, dust you off and help you home.

SUGRIVA: I will always love you, brother.

(VALI is stone-faced and silent. SUGRIVA nods.)

The will of the gods be done.

(The two collide with terrifying force. The fight is on. Their strokes are powerful, their blows deadly. They are equally matched in force but soon, SUGRIVA begins to tire. VALI strikes him three times. SUGRIVA's knees buckle. RAMA steps out from where he was hidden, and places a

quiver in his bow. He looks behind him. Is it SITA watching him from the shadows?)

RAMA: Sita?

SITA: My soul – I am here to watch over your dharma. I have known this since I first saw you at the river, washing blood from your hands.

RAMA: Sugriva has enough Vanaras to cover the earth's face searching for you. I will do what must be done.

(In one move, he shoots VALI through the heart. The powerful monkey-man falls to the earth with thunderous impact. SUGRIVA moves to his dying brother's side. He lies gasping, blood flowing from his mouth. RAMA kneels in prayer. The spectre of SITA walks slowly away. RAMA takes VALI in his arms.)

VALI: Have I died?

RAMA: You are going, Great One. But not yet gone.

VALI: My life becomes a thin and fading thing. Is it you – Blue One of Grace – that holds me at the gateway?

RAMA: It is Rama who holds you, and Rama who killed you, my friend.

VALI: *(In disbelief.)* You took it upon yourself to string your bow with my death… *(Overcome with emotion.)* Is it true – Rama of Impeccable Dharma?

RAMA: It is you that has broken Dharma, monkey king.

(SUGRIVA weeps silently at VALI's side, but VALI stares only at RAMA – as though he is seeing a vision. RAMA begins to glow incandescently. It is VALI's dying image of him.)

VALI: *(Smiling.)* Ah! Look…

SUGRIVA: *(Seeing his brother's face luminous with vision.)* What do you see, brother?

VALI: I see my way out of this broken body. Realms opening that were hidden from me before. You give me a path out of the bondage of this broken body – now that I know, dark prince, who you are.

RAMA: Who I am?

VALI: Yes! *(VALI is smiling, lost in his vision and slipping away.)*

RAMA: WHO?

(But VALI only turns to SUGRIVA with a gentle smile.)

VALI: We will meet again, brother. Look for me. I am there.

(VALI exhales for a last time and dies. SUGRIVA kneels and holds VALI. He weeps over the empty body of his brother. Thunder rumbles in the ever-darkening sky. RAMA is deeply shaken.)

SUGRIVA: I will wait always at life's cave for you – until my own end.

HANUMAN: *(To RAMA and LAKSHMANA.)* The Monsoons are come. I will show you our cave beneath the mountains where you will pass these months until the rains end.

RAMA: I will be waiting word from Sugriva that he has found where my Sita is held. I ache for the future… But this is the waiting season. May the gods give me strength.

SUGRIVA: *(SUGRIVA lifts VALI's body and carries it into the driving rain.)* Come with me brother. It's time to go home.

(SUGRIVA roars with grief, as the sky explodes with rain.)

VII.

(RAVANA is slumped in his throne, with a hand over his eyes. His son INDRAJIT stands beside him. Enter VIBHEESHANA.)

VIBHEESHANA: Brother, may I approach?

(RAVANA – without uncovering his eyes – nods. VIBHEESHANA moves in.)

Rama has created a powerful alliance with the Vanaras under Sugriva…

INDRAJIT: You are mistaken. The Vanaras are ruled by Vali.

VIBHEE: No longer. Rama of Ayhoda has slain Vali and placed Sugriva back on the throne.

(RAVANA looks up astonished, but gathers himself immediately.)

RAVANA: And in return for this "magnanimous" deed?

VIBHEE: Sugriva has sworn to avenge those who stole The Blue Prince's woman.

RAVANA: And Rama of Ayhoda is where?

VIBHEE: He awaits news in an undisclosed cave until the Monsoons end. It is said he who took his woman will know the white flame of his wrath.

(RAVANA mocks a shudder and smiles at his son. INDRAJIT laughs – searching his father's face.)

VIBHEE: Tell me brother: Is she worth it?

(RAVANA looks up sharply.)

– That you would allow the black song of doubt to enter your closest consorts. That they whisper amongst themselves "Ravana is drowning, like a woman, in sentiment and courts his own death". Is she worth your death?

RAVANA: *(Dropping all sarcasm.)* Brother, she recalls in me the dark lullabies of our mother's despair. I drift towards the end of the ravine with my eyes closed. I float. I fall into dark waters. I must have what lives beneath there.

INDRAJIT: *(Deeply unnerved.)* Why does my father – Lord of all the Worlds – not simply TAKE what is his?

(RAVANA breathes deeply, closes his eyes and is quiet. VIBHEESHANA stares at him, seeing the truth.)

VIBHEE: *(Understanding, for the first time, just how lost his brother is.)* Because your father is cursed never to force himself on a woman again.
Besides… lust alone is not what this is…

(RAVANA looks at his brother, startled at being exposed – and then surrenders, closing his eyes again.)

INDRAJIT: *(Urgently, beginning to lose control.)* Father, she will never love you. But there is no reason to lose everything simply because she resists. Your longing is simply desire thwarted. You yourself taught me this. Enter her daily – violently – until, to you, she is any other whore. There is nothing like lust sated…to break the Sentimental Spell.

VIBHEE: *(Raising his voice to INDRAJIT.)* THIS IS THE WIFE OF RAMA OF AYHODA! Not some CHILD of war your father has orphaned, with whom he can now do as he will!

INDRAJIT: *(Stunned by VIBHEESHANA's tone.)* Mind yourself, old man. You forget who I am.

VIBHEE: *(Treading carefully, for INDRAJIT is indeed powerful.)* I forget nothing, glorious warrior. But let there be no doubt… Yama waits in the shadows of this longing.

INDRAJIT: Sita will soon burn for his touch – like all the Whores that came before. But what would you know of such things, uncle? You are not like the men of our line. You have always carried the compassion of a woman. How convenient to be afforded such luxury: We must walk the battle fields, while you languish in moral dilemma at home!

VIBHEE: Hear me. Sita is the fire that will consume Lanka. Her husband comes in upon us from a timeless void borne of ages we will never master or know.

INDRAJIT: You speak with Indrajit – named so when he conquered the King of the Devas. If Rama of Ayhoda ever finds these shores – he will face me and he will know my true name.

VIBHEE: Rama of Lanka will tutor you in what I and even your father cannot.

INDRAJIT: He is a mortal. WE are Rakshasas. Do you forget what this means?

RAVANA: Meghanada –

INDRAJIT: It has been a long time since you have used my original name.

RAVANA: Meghanada – whose birth cry sounded like thunder. *(Lost in his thoughts, barely listening to his son and brother's conversation.)*

INDRAJIT: How can I serve my Father... My King?

(RAVANA beckons him to come close. He bends to catch RAVANA's soft words.)

RAVANA: I will have her eyes change just once for me, the way they do when she speaks his name. Do this for me. Destroy what stands in love's way.

INDRAJIT: *(Desperately, with rage.)* Father...

(But RAVANA has withdrawn again, hand over his eyes. VIBHEESHANA leads INDRAJIT away.)

VIBHEE: He is lost.
Ready all that can possibly hold back the tide that will soon move in.

VIII.

(RAMA lies on his back in a cave listening to the storm raging outside. The SITA-BODY moves around him as a shadow, then lays full length on him. He starts awake. LAKSHMANA is sleeping at his side. Time passes. Water drips in the cave as the seconds, hours, weeks, months pass. All the while, the monsoons fall powerfully outside. RAMA strikes the wall and cries out at the pain. LAKSHMANA sits up and watches him.)

LAKSHMANA: Be patient brother...

RAMA: *(Beginning to lose control.)* Where is she, brother? With whom does she spend her nights?

LAKSHMANA: Sugriva has surely sent his vanaras through the three worlds to find her. We will soon have news.

RAMA: I don't have the strength for doing nothing, brother.

LAKSHMANA: *(Coming to him with infinite compassion, he holds him by his shoulders.)* We cannot know why – but there is an enemy whom destiny has set against you.
Sita is the river that draws us all towards a battlefield for reasons larger than your love – for we are instruments of the Dharma. No more or less.
Now let us think only of finding her – and bring her home.

RAMA: *(Gathering himself.)* My brother, my soul's friend…
Finest amongst all men.

(RAMA embraces LAKSHMANA. They step back and look at each other as the world turns.)

IX.

(SUGRIVA lies inebriated in the stupor of wine. HANUMAN prods him awake.)

HANUMAN: You have your kingdom back, your wife, your life. You swore to Rama you would begin when the monsoons had passed! My Lord – what keeps you?

SUGRIVA: *(Drunk.)* And have they passed, Son of the Wind? I am certain I still hear water's feet dancing pitter pat along the roof.

HANUMAN: The moon hangs low in a clear sky. It has been peaceful Sharada for more than a month. While you have been happy at wine and love, Rama counts not the seasons – but each moment of his life that passes without his beloved. Now is the time to call our Vanaras to comb the face of the earth for Rama's wife!

SUGRIVA: I need yet time to climb back into the world.

HANUMAN: I would not delay, my Lord. Lest Rama's love turn to rage.

(SUGRIVA looks frightened but does not move.)

SUGRIVA: It has been many grievous years of waiting to come home. I am taking the time to heal, Hanuman.

HANUMAN: A warrior with death on his brow has arrived in our city. Lakshmana – brother to Rama of Ayhoda waits at the gate.

(SUGRIVA's smile fades. He grows very still.)

SUGRIVA: Show him in.

(SUGRIVA rises from his bed. LAKSHMANA enters. He stands silently – pale with rage.)

VALMIKI 2: "The body is not me and I not the body" the truth whispers. But gets lost all the same. "How beautiful is the song of wine and women?" she whispers, as we fall into the dark embrace.

LAKSHMANA: *(Quietly, with deadly rage.)* The portal through which Vali left this world is yet open for you to follow. Honour your promise, before despair becomes my master and I kill you, Vanara.

(SUGRIVA begins to weep. He prostrates himself before LAKSHMANA, touching his feet.)

SUGRIVA: Now you see the limits of the monkey-mind. Forgive me – I beg you. I cannot be what I am not.

LAKSHMANA: You gave Rama your word.
We of the Ishvaku line – hold nothing deeper than giving our word.

SUGRIVA: *(SUGRIVA, now fully lucid to the failed promises he made, turns to HANUMAN.)* Summon my Vanaras from every jungle's corner. Those who do not come will die. *(To LAKSHMANA.)* I will not fail your brother again. We will find his Sita – or may the Vanaras be cursed to search without pause – to the end of time.

X.

(RAVANA stands over SITA, looking down at her on the floor of the cell. She does not look at him but chants her Vedas repeatedly, rocking and looking into the cupped palms of her hands, held close to her face.)

RAVANA: *(Inhaling deeply.)* I smell you. I want you. More than any woman I have known in this realm.

(SITA will not look at him.)

You don't know what it is to be in my embrace, Sita. Taste me. I will give you my all.

(She quietly continues chanting the vedas.)

Many have longed to capture my dark heart… But you scorn it!

(Suddenly, he grabs her and drags her to her feet, through his halls and to a window where the ocean roars below.)

All of this...I give it to you.

(Though she is shaking violently, she has a calm smile on her lips. He grasps her from behind and forces her face towards the magnificent view of Lanka.)

I am the Emperor of ten million Rakshasas across the earth. All of them will be your subjects. You will have glory and power beyond your dreams. The thousand pieces of my harem shall be your handmaids. I will never touch one of them again if you ask this of me.

(He falls to his knees in front of her. She remains unmoved. He covers his ears.)

It is a childhood song I hear, since I first saw you, before waking.
My mother entering and leaving a room as cold as your heart.
I want to lie in your arms and weep until sleeping.

SITA: *(She looks him in the eyes for the first time. She moves in closer.)* What you do not know – Rakshasa – is that you are looking at your own death.

RAVANA: *(They hold each other's stare. Then quietly – with his own lethal power.)* You have 100 days to consider my love. If you accept – you will be Queen of the three worlds. If you refuse –

(His ten heads appear. It is a grotesque and awesome sight. SITA is struck dumb.)

I will bring pain your fragile body has never known. I will take you as mine – so violently that your insides will bleed from every portal your body owns.

SITA: It is known you are cursed never to force yourself on a woman again.

RAVANA: *(Smiling darkly.)* But I love you, you see. How may I show you the lengths I am willing to go to? I will dance in the dark face of this curse. If its my last act of violence in this world, I will tear into you – body and soul.

SITA: You will be ash, Rakshasa, when you face the power of my vratas!

Do what you will. The soul is untouchable. And this body is but a passing thing.

(RAVANA grabs SITA and pulls her towards him but he is unhinged. He throws her to the ground. To his own astonishment, he finds his face wet with tears.)

RAVANA: Don't look at me. *(He roars with rage.)* LOOK AWAY! *(She looks down – for he is ferocious.)* By love or by force – in a hundred days – your body is mine.

(He turns and leaves her alone. VIBHEESHANA, his brother, is waiting for him on the other side of the door.)

VIBHEESH: Brother, this is part of some larger design! Whoever convinced you that you could steal Rama of Ayhoda's wife – wants you...wants all of us...Dead.

(RAVANA turns. VIBHEESHANA calls after him.)

Ravana! RAVANA! *(But RAVANA walks away without turning back.)*

XI.

(HANUMAN sits staring into the swelling tides of the ocean. An eagle spirals above him. It is DASARATHA, RAMA's father, who flies the eagle. In her cell, SITA stands. Her eyes are closed but she stretches her arms above her as though she sees the eagle in her dream. It lands near HANUMAN and speaks through DASARATHA.)

DAS as SAMPATI: Son of the Wind, what do you wait on the shores of doubt for?

HANUMAN: Great One. I would rather die than return to Rama with no news of the Devi.

DASARATHA as SAMPATI: She is prisoner to Ravana – Lord of the Rakshasas. He keeps her in in the City of Lanka, in his favourite Askovana.

HANUMAN: *(Astonished.)* How do you know this?

DASARATHA as SAMPATI: My Brother, Jataya, died defending Sita. Go now, before it is too late. Her time is almost at an end.

HANUMAN: *(Desperately.)* But how will I reach her? An ocean lies between me and Lanka.

SITA as SAMPATI: Why, Sun of the Wind, do you doubt yourself so much? *(Simply.)* Jump!

HANUMAN: *(Laughing in disbelief.)* Jump?
You regard me too highly, Great One.

SITA as SAMPATI: You have forgotten who you are, Vayuputra! As a child, you leapt into the sky because you thought the sun a succulent orange to devour! Indra flung a thunderbolt that merely grazed your cheek. When was it, Invincible One, that you became so afraid?

VALMIKI 1: Remembering ourselves on the long dust road – who among us would not rather forget and fold back into fear? But we are ever called to spread arms and free-fall into the fearless children we were once ordained to be.

(HANUMAN stands tall, as though the bonds of fear are falling from him like great chains coming apart. He roars.)

HANUMAN: There was a time once, that I carried the moon in these hands around the earth. I could tear Lanka up by its roots if I wished – and bring Sita to Rama still on Lanka's soil. *(HANUMAN crouches and readies himself. Then roaring – he launches himself upwards into the sky.)*

VALMIKI 2: Sitting on the shores of doubt – like dry wood waiting for kindling, the flame ignites. With a leap of faith, we are borne into the wind towards our true way.

4. Crossing Over

I.

(RAVANA's halls are silent – but for the breathing of slumber and the soporific swell of the ocean below. The plastic on the scaffolding billows and deflates. RAVANA twists in dreams, his magnificent dark form naked and laid with scars. MANDODARI sleeps soundly nearby. HANUMAN tiptoes through the halls. He stops and looks over the sleeping woman's face.)

HANUMAN: *(Whispering.)* Sita?

(MANDODARI stirs and mutters in her sleep. HANUMAN sees that though this woman's beauty fits RAMA's description, she is older than SITA could be.)

(He shrinks away as RAVANA groans softly and rises. HANUMAN follows RAVANA into the askovana, where he stands watching SITA sleep. He looks haunted and strangely vanquished. HANUMAN hides in the shadows. SITA sits up in fear.)

RAVANA: Rise from this cold, dust floor, and take your rightful place beside me as my Queen.

SITA: *(Looking him in the eyes.)* Have you no one that cares for you here? Are they all too afraid to tell you: You will die Rakshasa! We are more than you will ever know.

RAVANA: It is known across the three worlds: I am invincible, my dear.

SITA: Are you?

RAVANA: Ten thousand years of perfect worship – for which Siva, God of Gods, granted me immortality…

SITA: Beware the man who believes he has God on his side.

RAVANA: No Deva, Danava, Daitya, Asura, Rakshasa, gandharva, kinnara, charana, siddha can touch me. Neither divine nor demonic beings can harm or end my life.

SITA: But in your arrogance, you forgot to ask invincibility from mortals, Rakshasa.

RAVANA: If I am immortal against the Devas – I assume *(He smiles.)* this will protect me from your soft prince, who has known nothing but privilege all his life.

SITA: *(Looking deeply into his eyes.)* Doom is coming to Lanka. You cannot imagine the love Rama enfolds me in. It will make of your city – ash. Do you not feel the shadows move this way?

(RAVANA smiles.)

RAVANA: Are you trying to frighten the Lord of the Rakshasas?

SITA: I pity you.

RAMA: Save your pity. I am a brutal man.

SITA: You claim to have conquered thousands of women – yet you know nothing of our sex. Were I never promised to Rama, I would still rather die than give myself to you. No one has the courage to say it…but you are grotesque, Rakshasa.

Anyone…ANYONE could have me before you.

(RAVANA's fists are closing with rage – but SITA pushes on with great scorn.)

When Rama's arrow is buried to its feathers in your black heart know how sad and impotent you truly are – you will

(For a long moment, RAVANA grows very still. In an instant he draws his sword and stands over her – weapon poised to decapitate her. SITA raises her face to his and gazes calmly into his eyes. They are locked in a silent struggle of wills. HANUMAN is about to reveal himself and intervene – but MANDODARI is suddenly behind RAVANA. She does not look at SITA. She wraps her arms around RAVANA's neck.)

MANDODARI: The Harem is empty without you. I wait every night for you to come and enjoy new beauties captured but not yet tasted – from unknown realms. Our bodies burn for you. Come, husband, and let us take your anguish from you.

(RAVANA slowly backs away, though he does not take his eyes from SITA. Finally he allows himself to be led away. MANDODARI and SITA's

eyes briefly meet. MANDODARI nods and turns away. Alone, SITA sits quietly – drained. HANUMAN, remaining concealed lest he frighten SITA, begins to chant in Sanskrit, the narrative of RAMA and SITA's story. SITA stands stunned. SITA stands perfectly still. She closes her eyes and listens to her own history unfold. Gently, HANUMAN emerges from where he has been hiding and prostrates himself before her.

HANUMAN: Whose feet do I touch?

SITA: They call me Sita in this life.

HANUMAN: Devi – your Rama sent me to you.

SITA: *(Stunned.)* My Rama?

(HANUMAN moves towards her in empathy. SITA shrinks from him and cries out.)

If you are Ravana in another form…

(HANUMAN lays his face at her feet. SITA watches him for awhile, but he remains still. Slowly he holds a ring up to her.)

Rama said to give you this ring that you would know he sent me…

(She tentatively takes it and looks at it. Tears flow when she finds it to be RAMA's. She falls to her knees.)

SITA: Who are you?

HANUMAN: My people call me Hanuman, Devi.

(HANUMAN, with great humility, bows before her.)

SITA: Forgive me for having doubted you, Hanuman. My faith has been worn thin. The Rakshasa will have me at all costs if I do not submit by full moon after next. I wait and pray. I don't know what more to do.

HANUMAN: You will not see another moon in Lanka, Devi.

SITA: But how will an entire army cross the ocean that lies between Rama and me?

HANUMAN: Be at peace, Devi…

SITA: The unthinkable had crossed my mind that Rama no longer...

(She can't go on.)

HANUMAN: *(Quietly.)* Before his eyes open each morning, he is uttering your name. Like a prayer. At night, "Sita" is his mantra over and under his tongue, until he sleeps.

(SITA sits on the bare earth and, for the first time, allows her grief to take its full force.)

SITA: All this suffering is the karma of previous lives untold.

HANUMAN: Ravana will know his karma sooner than he can dream.

SITA: *(She turns to him. Her face is dark with thought.)* Hanuman, I am a branch severed from my own life. Soon – I fear – I will be dead.

HANUMAN: Devi, I am the son of the wind. Climb on my back. I will cross the yawning sea and bring you to Rama this night!

SITA: *(Shaking her head gently but with immovable conviction.)* Vayuputra, Ravana's powers reach father and deeper than we can imagine. Rama must come to Lanka to fight this dharma yuddha – and end Ravana's reign. What is my discomfort in the face of this holy war that must be fought time and time again?

HANUMAN: You are truly Rama of Ayhoda's wife.

SITA: *(But she is distracted.)* Before the moon returns to the nakshatra he must come for me, Hanuman... Or we will never see each other in this lifetime again.

(HANUMAN looks at her, startled. He knows this is not said lightly.)

HANUMAN: Devi, how might I prove to Rama that I saw you?

SITA: *(Her eyes fill with tears, though she smiles.)* Speak to him of the time we were caught together in a sudden rain, and my tilaka was rubbed away. I lay my head in his lap when we found shelter in a cave. He took the dust of the mansila stone, kissed my brow gently and marked it. Then he spoke of the sons we would someday have. No one else could know about those hours we shared in that cavern alone.

(HANUMAN prostrates himself at SITA's feet. She blesses him. He stands.) I will not survive here beyond the next lunar month. I hope we meet again Vayuputra.

HANUMAN: Have no doubt, Devi. Before the moon returns to the nakshatra.

(HANUMAN bows deeply, turns and is gone.)

SITA: *(Opening her palms and talking to RAMA as though he were present.)* I have been lost my love. But dreamed of you last night. Your body on the timeless ocean, drifting toward me over great circles of pain. I came to you weeping.

You took my hand and we began to walk the dark waters. Even into the great sleep you were there – by my side.

(We see RAMA kneeling on the shore line beneath a full moon, facing Lanka. He rises and arches his back, giving his heart towards the light. With his eyes closed, he calls out her name.)

II.

(RAVANA and his councilors surround HANUMAN – who is bound with ropes and curled on the floor. They turn him over. He gasps at the terrible beauty of RAVANA's ten heads.)

HANUMAN: Ravana of Lanka, how magnificent you truly are.

RAMA: *(Locking eyes with HANUMAN, he hisses to VIBHEESHANA beside him.)* Who is he? What does he want?

(The ten heads extend further from the neck in curiosity and smoldering rage.)

HANUMAN: I am myself. In true form – a Vanara. No astra may bind me.

(He draws the ropes away from his body as though he were breaking fragile string.)

I allowed myself to be captured because I wished to meet you face to faces. *(He smiles at his little joke.)* Listen to my words and they may profit you – dark one.

(RAVANA says nothing but watches HANUMAN and waits.)

She is the fire of truth you kindle. She will make of your city a wasteland of ash.

RAVANA: *(In a low growl.)* Kill him.

VIBHEESHANA: My Lord – to kill the messenger is not dharma.

RAVANA: Have I not tolerated insults in a way that no King would?

VIBHEESHANA: Send an army against the human prince. A great warrior knows when not to strike. Let them say that Ravana spared the messanger's life –

(RAVANA's eyes flicker with rage – but the ten heads nod with calculation.)

RAVANA: Set his tail alight, and then release him. I can think of no message more articulate for Rama than the burnt stump on your Vanara behind! BRING ME FIRE!

HANUMAN's tail is wrapped and dipped in oil.

As they touch fire to it – he turns to RAVANA.

HANUMAN: She is your death, magnificent one. And you will know it soon.

(HANUMAN leaps from where he stands – and with his tail blazing, tears through Lanka.)

SITA: *(Stepping out of her current horror to reflect.)* Hanuman lit the city of Lanka that night, as he ran across the roof tops, harvesting destruction wherever he went. He looked back once over his shoulder, jumped the ocean and with him – took my soul home

(KUSA and LAVA begin to sing, and we see HANUMAN beside RAMA once again, telling him all that occurred. He points across the sea into the distance. RAMA embraces HANUMAN fiercely and then stares out over the vast waters towards his love.)

SITA: I stood amidst the flames of presence that night, beloved. I kept the heat at bay by inviting it in. But mothers and children burnt alive in their homes, where they had lain down to sleep in each other's arms. I will hold always in my heart, their unforgettable screams. Let us never forget: Pain is sown and harvested, my beloved, wherever the black boot of war goes.

III.

(RAMA sits on the shore in prayopavesha. LAKSHMANA sits beside him – also in prayer.)

VALMIKI 1: With a singleness of thought we sit the silence and wait to cross the vast and ambitious sea of self.

(RAMA turns to LAKSHMANA.)

RAMA: Bring me my bow.

(LAKSHMANA brings RAMA his bow. RAMA fits an arrow and then assuming alidha, he roars like an angry God.)

If the gentle way will not be heard – I will open with force what remains closed to me here.

VALMIKI 1: The sky grows dark as Midnight. We stand like a flame upon the shore, as a great lament rises from the ocean, filled with ancient grief.

RAMA: VARUNA! I will consume you. I will make ash of your acres. Vast plains of desert with no memory that they once held water. I will cross into Lanka over your parched mountain ranges that sit now in dark waters below.

VALMIKI 2: The sun and moon stray from their orbits. Chaos verges on the inner world. And then the ocean recedes, as Varuna Deva – body of water and light – strides toward the shore.

(The Sea – SITA-BODY as water – prostrates itself at RAMA's feet.)

SITA-BODY as VARUNA: Lord, it is the pristine and unbroken nature of the sun to shine; the wind to blow; the earth to turn. Not even I can still the waves that flow from me. Like you – I cannot be what I am not.

RAMA: You are in my way Varuna! And if I am ever to find my heart again – you must be crossed. I will decimate you and all life within you, if you do not give way.

VARUNA: I cannot be destroyed, Blue One. Find your way over my icy miles of fear and then I give you my word: As you and your untamed vanaras cross my waters...whatever way you find to achieve this – I will hold you in my arms.

(The sound of grief becomes the breath of the ocean once more.)

SUGRIVA: Shall we begin, my Lord?

RAMA: Begin...?

SUGRIVA: The work. The sacred bridge we must build across these waves to bring us to Lanka.

RAMA: How is this possible, Sugriva?

SUGRIVA: We are a magical people, Lord. The vanaras have ranged the earth since the beginning of time. There is much work to be done...

(RAMA nods silently like a child and drops to his knees. SUGRIVA gives an ancient war cry, calling the Vanaras to begin their sacred task.)

IV.

(RAVANA moves through the ashes of Lanka. Everywhere, HANUMAN has left destruction in his wake. RAVANA faces the audience – amongst whom sits INDRAJIT his son; VIBHEESHANA his brother and councilors. He addresses the audience as though addressing his own Senate. MANDODARI stands silently nearby.)

RAVANA: *(He pauses to gather his power and then looks directly at his senate.)* I come to you for council, for we will soon be at war. Are we ready to show The Blue Prince and his Monkeys that we intend to rule for another age?

(The room echos with the roars of the RAKSHASAS. Suddenly a lone voice speaks.)

VIBHEESHANA: My brother, hear me! I alone love you in this sabha. For I alone will tell you the truth: Return Sita at Rama's side, or we are all doomed.

(Turning to the council of RAKSHASAS, RAVANA roars.)

RAVANA: I am Ravana of Lanka. My valour is as deep as the ocean. I am as strong as Vayu. Do I look doomed to you?

(The RAKSHASAS roar in response.)

VIBHEESHANA: You hunger as a man – yet will destroy like a child – whatever stands in the way of making Rama's wife your queen.

(RAVANA turns with blazing eyes to his brother. All look to MANDODARI, but she keeps her face blank, as inscrutable as ever.)

The price has already been considerable! Rama's Monkey has left our city in ash. An army of Vanaras are headed towards our gates. Your woman troubles will end us all!

INDRAJIT: How dare you?

VIBHEESHANA: I say this not to humiliate you, brother. But to prevent your untimely death.

INDRAJIT: Rama of Ayhoda is not a god but a man. The weakest among us could kill this mortal prince.

(VIBHEESHANA smiles with patronizing but genuine pity at INDRAJIT.)

VIBHEESHANA: You are young, Meghanada – and though you are already a legend on the battle field – you are a boy. You should not be here amongst your elders. You are yet a boy.

(Blazing with rage, INDRAJIT opens his mouth to retaliate – but VIBHEESHANA simply turns from him, back to RAVANA.)

Return Sita to her husband's side and beg on broken knees before The Blue Prince. Then come home in peace to Lanka, and rule for another age. Ask forgiveness from Rama of Ayhoda or Lanka is surely doomed.

RAVANA: *(RAVANA turns to his brother, smiling and eyes burning with rage.)* Never.

(Everyone roars with approval.)

VIBHEESHANA: *(Turning to the Senate.)* Show him your love, Rakshasas, by stopping him. Use any means necessary. He cannot save his own life.

RAVANA: *(In a terrifying rage.)* You are an enemy to Lanka from this day forward.

VIBHEESHANA: These very Rakshasas who urge you forward today will soon be silenced.
Their brave bodies, rotting flesh for scavenger birds by tomorrow's setting sun.

(His eyes glistening with tears.)

Forgive me, brother. I wanted only to save your life.
We will not meet in peace in this lifetime again.

(VIBHEESHANA rises and walks out of the assembly – leaving the council in stunned silence.)

V.

VALMIKI 1: Finally we must all traverse the bridge between what we know and where we have no choice but to go.

(RAMA stands on the completed bridge the Vanaras built. He makes a ritual blessing. They look up into the distance, and along the bridge from Lanka – comes VIBHEESHANA. He prostrates himself before him.)

RAMA: Who is at my feet?

VIBHEESHANA: Brother to Ravana of Lanka.

(LAKSHMANA and SUGRIVA look to one another stunned, hands on their weapons. HANUMAN recalls VIBHEESHANA from his night in Lanka and stands, quietly observing him.)

I am branded a traitor and banished, my Lord.

LAKSHMANA: *(With his weapon in hand.)* Why?

VIBHEESHANA: I will not lie to you, Rama of Ayhoda. I love my brother. I wanted to save his life. But he would not hear my pleas to return Sita to your side.

LAKSHMANA: Do you come alone?

VIBHEESHANA: I have abandoned even my wives and children in Lanka – though I know they are doomed. I come to serve in whatever way I can.

SUGRIVA: We cannot risk this.

(RAMA looks at LAKSHMANA.)

LAKSHMANA: I wait your decision. If you declare him friend, I will embrace him with my heart. Name him Enemy – and I will kill him without a moment's pause.

RAMA: *(Looking to HANUMAN who waits quietly.)* Hanuman?

HANUMAN: *(Quietly.)* Vibheeshana spoke for my life in Ravana's sabha when death was certain. He has chosen the way of the dharma over his own flesh and blood. What further proof could be asked but the abandonment of all he loves?

SUGRIVA: This is a Rakshasa, Lord Rama. Lying is their way. Betrayal – their song.

VIBHEESHANA: *(He prostrates himself at Rama's feet again.)* My life is yours.

(All wait to know VIBHEESHANA's fate.)

RAMA: The way of the dharma is clear on this: No one who seeks sanctuary should ever be turned away.

(He lays his hand gently on the Rakshasa's head. VIBHEESHANA begins to weep.)

You are embraced as brother to us all.

(RAMA helps him rise. LAKSHMANA, SUGRIVA and HANUMAN unreservedly each embrace VIBHEESHANA in turn.)

RAMA: *(To LAKSHMANA.)* Bring us water from the sea. We will crown this brother King of the Rakshasas. Those who survive what is coming to Lanka, will need someone to rule.

(LAKSHMANA gathers water from the shore. RAMA anoints VIBHEESHANA. They stand on the bridge, looking across the waters as daylight begins to fade.)

Tomorrow, brave Vanaras and Rakshasas will lie dead side by side – their lives extinguished on Lanka's shores. Their blood will colour the earth. And my heart breaks for us all.

(The women around the SITA-BODY stretch her out once more, and one by one, they kiss her brow and sing of loss and war. LAKSHMANA,

RAMA, VIBHEESHANA, SUGRIVA and HANUMAN walk away on the windswept beach, as VIBHEESHANA shares the secrets of Lanka.)

VIBHEESHANA: Like your native Ayhoda – there are Nine Gates by which one can breach our city wall…

VALMIKI 2: Nine points of entry. As it always was, and will be, in matters of the heart.

(The women gathered around the SITA-BODY, massage the heart area and turn her onto her side.)

VI.

(SITA sits in her cell – fervently chanting the Vedas. In his chamber, RAVANA is woken by INDRAJIT.)

INDRAJIT: Father, wake up! Rama and his monkeys have reached our shores.

RAVANA: Impossible.

INDRAJIT: They will soon be at the city gates. Your Rakshasas wait to hear from you.

(RAVANA rises with urgency disguised as fury and moves to the window to address his RAKSHASAS below.)

RAVANA: You dare stand before me – trembling like virgins in my Harem!
(Roaring.) HAVE YOU FORGOTTEN WHO WE ARE?
(The RAKSHASAS roar.)

RAMA: *(Suddenly from the Northern Gate.)* You could have been King of the Devas! It is YOU, Rakshasa, who has forgotten who you are!

(RAVANA looks out into the early morning to see RAMA standing on the wall. At last they face each other.)

You offered the world a gift when you stole my wife. For now Rama of Ayhoda is at your city gates, and the hour of retribution is come. Return Sita to me; and save countless lives.

(The VALMIKIS are at the feet and head of the SITA-BODY. They will both offer accounts of what comes next, using the body like a map, a land on which the war will ensue. They will mark it with diagrams, write words on it, run their hands over it. The SITA-BODY is lit to look like the undulating hills and plains of Lanka .)

VALMIKI 2: Countless Rakshasas – armed to the teeth – stare out at an ocean of Vanaras, waiting to storm their nine gates.

RAMA: What do you say Ravana? There is yet time to turn this around.

(RAVANA smiles.)

RAVANA: *(Smiling.)* No wonder she loves you, beautiful Rama. Your heart shines like time.

VALMIKI 1: Rama turns to his monkey men and simply nods. The roar is deafening as vanaras surge forward, each monkey determined to be the first over Lanka's walls.

(The VALMIKIS use the SITA-BODY to tell the story of the coming war. The powerful song of LAVA and KUSA, and the singing from the VALMIKIS at the SITA-BODY, alternately score the war narrative throughout.)

VALMIKI 2: What mathematics of time and fate have brought each warrior to this battlefield to face Yamma's gates? Only the gods know and they are silent, as blood flows and the plan follows its invisible design.

VALMIKI 1: Tar black blood glistens on Lanka's fields like dark dew. The Rakshasas are ferocious but Sugriva's monkey brethren plough through exhaustion and cry out with renewed strength under the rising moon.

(RAMA and LAKSHMANA stand centre, side by side – releasing their bows with awe-inspiring prowess.)

VALMIKI 2: Not an arrow of Rama and Lakshmana's fails to claim a Rakshasa life. After 13 hours of relentless battle, the Rakshasas flee the mighty Vanara storm.

VII.

(RAVANA sits hissing on his throne like a serpent. Even his own ministers cannot bear the sight of him. INDRAJIT enters and approaches his father.)

INDRAJIT: Take some wine, father. And some women for the night. Let history smile through the ages, that when the Vanaras came to Lanka's gates, the Great Ravana did not get to his feet. His son took care of The Blue Prince alone.

(INDRAJIT turns swiftly and in a deft move, is out onto the battle field. The Rakshasas roar: Jaya Indrajit! Jaya!.)

VALMIKI 2: Indrajit was born with war in his veins. Preparation for battle was an experience never matched for him by any women. At the edge of the field now, he kindles a fire and worships the Navagraha, the nine planets, the sacred fire.

(INDRAJIT performs his legendary Yagna in preparation for battle. He chants mantras. When the ceremony is concluded, he speaks to his gods.)

INDRAJIT: I am Indrajit, who conquered the king of the Devas! Bring me Rama of Ayhoda. And his pale brother. In my father's name – I will have them both.

VALMIKI 1: In a deadly battle for their Yuvaraja, the Vanaras fight with ferocity. But Lanka's son brings the ancient craft of "Maya" to those death fields today.

VALMIKI 2: Filling the skies with visions so exquisite, the monkeys cannot tear their eyes from the beauty of death as it falls like deadly rain.

RAMA: *(To LAKSHMANA at his side, watching the extraordinary weapons of Maya.)* It is Brahma's mysteries he invokes. He wants us to run in fear. He does not know whom he faces today.

VALMIKI 1: Whispering – the fiery blossoms gently tumble towards the monkey army, whose faces are turned up in awe like children watching the monsoon storms. And one by one, every monkey falls into the halls of waiting, where only Yamma calls.

RAMA: *(Calling out to LAKSHMANA.)* They are held in the blossoms' deadly power. Call the brahmana's trance away from the forest people to us. Against it – only we may stand a chance.

(RAMA and LAKSHMANA draw the deadly blossom towards themselves and fall deep into coma. In the dense darkness that has fallen – we hear a beautiful chanting. The only thing visible is the SITA-BODY – though covered in the marks of war – shining with incandescent light.)

VALMIKI 1: Dreams of Brahmaloka draw the brothers far from the bloodied fields of Lanka, and into realms they must forget when they wake… If they ever do. For the torpor of the brahmastra is said to last until the universe vanishes in the pralaya. And then everything must, painstakingly, atom by atom, begin once again.

(A match is lit. VIBHEESHANA stands holding out a small flame. A lone torch slowly weaves its way towards him. He sees it is HANUMAN approaching. They embrace fiercely.)

VIBHEESH: Brahma truly blessed you that his own powers are useless against you!

HANUMAN: *(Falling to his knees when he sees his Lord and brother lying unconscious at his feet.)* RAMA! LAKSHMANA!

VIBHEESH: Do not despair, Hanuman! The Prince's are beneath death's mountain – but not yet dead.

HANUMAN: Lost in Brahmaloka! How will we ever bring them back?

VIBHEESH: As long as Hanuman lives – there is hope!

HANUMAN: *(Looking at VIBHEESHANA incredulously.)* Brother. What good is my body's strength, in the search for Rama – lost in the void from which no living thing returns?

VIBHEESH: Son of the Wind – it was never muscle and sinew alone that enabled you: It is what you are willing to give that saved us before and will save us now. Fly again for us, Heart of Devotion, across the ocean. Only you can save the Princes of Khosala and our fallen army.

HANUMAN: To where can I fly? I am lost.

VIBHEESHANA: In the north range of the Himalayas, miraculous plants of healing grow on the slopes of Oshadhiparvata. You will know the herbs by the soft light they shine with after dark. FLY Hanuman – and bring back these oshadis. With them I will raise our army from death's waiting chamber. I will be in the black night amongst our fallen, counting the hours until your return.

(HANUMAN opens his arms wide, exposing the heart area of his chest. He rises and flies into the night.)

5. Darkness

I.

(INDRAJIT sweeps into the cell where SITA sits chanting the vedas. She stops when he enters. It is the first time he has seen her. He is rocked to the core by her beauty. He reaches out slowly and runs a finger along her jaw and brow, down her neck – stopping short of going further.)

INDRAJIT: They did not lie. You are exquisite, Sita of Rama! I would have you myself...
But here in Lanka, we let our father's eat first, and are happy to suck like scavengers on bones, once our elders lie sated.

(SITA tries to cover herself, terrified. Whereas RAVANA is deeply in love with SITA, INDRAJIT emanates only pure, carnal lust. She turns away, chanting. INDRAJIT pulls RAMA's bow from behind his back and casts it in front of her. SITA looks up, frantically searching INDRAJIT's face.)

SITA: Where did you get this? Rama would never let you take it alive.

INDRAJIT: Exactly, beautiful one. I have felled Rama and his brother last night as a woodman might two young saplings.

SITA: I dreamt this.

INDRAJIT: Dead.

SITA: No...

INDRAJIT: Dead enough, sweet one. In a slumber that the gods themselves could not rise from – let alone two mortal men.

SITA: *(Turning inwards, whispering desperately into cupped hands.)* Is it true my love? Are you gone from this realm? The silken threads that hold us bound begin to strain. Are you still with me Rama?

(RAVANA is suddenly behind INDRAJIT, who immediately steps away in deference.)

RAVANA: You have eyes that see through time, Sita. You know he speaks the truth.

(SITA begins to rock herself, moaning – grief coming in vast waves.)

SITA: Rama, beloved. I feel breath but no heart beat. Heart beat but no breath. What if in the mountains of ages I must climb… I never find you again?

RAVANA: All your punya and your vratas could not protect them. Rise and ready yourself to be Queen!

SITA: *(Rocking, and whispering to RAMA between vedas.)* Into the chambers of your beating heart – I breathe life, Blue Prince. Lakshmana, wherever you both may be, find the portal back to this realm.

INDRAJIT: *(Grabbing her brutally by the hair and screaming into her face.)* The sands of our northern beaches are dark with monkey blood and faeces of fear. Your hermit boy is DEAD, whore!

(RAVANA, with one powerful and startling blow, strikes INDRAJIT from SITA. He reels – from shock rather than the pain – for he is more than RAVANA's equal in strength. But father and son have never been at odds before.)

RAVANA: She is my Queen. Mother to you soon. Touch her again or speak to her that way… And you will die by this hand that once held yours as a boy.

(INDRAJIT staggers back staring at RAVANA and SITA, his eyes stinging with tears. He turns and is gone. MANDODARI has been watching from the shadows. She steps in and looks deeply at SITA.)

RAVANA: You do not have my leave to be here, woman.

SITA: Who are you?

MANDODARI: *(She is overcome at the sight of SITA, but gathers herself seamlessly.)* You are beautiful, Sita.
And brave and true.
I understand now why he is willing to lose his kingdom, the love of his favourite son, his Queen…
For you –

(She reaches out and pulls the devastated SITA towards her.)

Leave her with me, Ravana. I will calm her as the women of your harem once calmed me. *(To SITA.)* Rest awhile child. You are safe for now, in my arms.

(She strokes SITA's hair. In her grief, SITA surrenders to this feminine, gentle touch. MANDODARI holds her against her breast rocking her, as she weeps. RAVANA watches them, curiously moved. He backs away, – leaving his Queen with the great love of his life. Once alone, MANDODARI's face is still but she silently weeps.)

II.

VALMIKI 1: As evening falls, Hanuman sees the Himalayas ahead of him. The slopes of the smallest peak glow with other worldly light. Hanuman grasps Oshadhiarvata by its sides, and tears that mountain's roots out of the earth. Body blazing, he does not stop until he reaches Rama's silent body in Lanka and places the mountain at his side.

(A mound of earth is placed on the belly of the SITA-BODY. A magnificent creature, GARUDA – half eagle, half man – circles above the unconscious RAMA.)

VALMIKI 1: In the weighty sleep of Nagpasa, Rama wonders: Is it my soul circling above – as it has done when it finally left the body in countless previous lives? I see my mother's eyes and long for her cool touch on the back of my neck when I was a boy. I feel my father near. His dark eyes looking for me when I would disappear into the shadowed gardens of home as a child. Is it you, father – come to call us back into the deep?

(GARUDA comes in for landing. DASARATHA flies him and speaks for him. He assumes a human form as he lands on earth – a manly physique – though his head is an eagle's and his wings are folded behind him.)

GARUDA: I am Garuda – your witness through the aeons. I can appear to you but once in each span of life. I bring word that neither the Devas nor gandharvas can lift the slumber in which you are bound. But Hanuman brings a mountain of devotion to your side. Fear nothing Future King. Ramaraja is soon here.

(RAMA and LAKSHMANA rise to their feet and watch the eagle circle and soar away.)

(RAVANA hears the cry of the eagle over the night's silence.)

RAVANA: *(To himself.)* It is not possible Dasartha's sons rise again! *(Roaring.)* Send every son I have to go among the legions. BRING ME THE KOSALA BROTHERS' HEARTS!

VALMIKI 2: The Rakshasas run full force towards the battle fields – fearless to pay with their lives. But the Vanaras have seen Rama rise from nagpasa tonight. They fight with joyous ferocity. Every Rakshasa, every son of Ravana's… falls.

(RAVANA stands in perfect stillness – his ten heads out in full rage.)

RAVANA: *(Fiercely.)* Ready me for battle! It is time.

III.

(RAMA is watching the Rakshasas sweep into battle from a distance. Suddenly he sees RAVANA's awesome figure in their midsts. He turns to VIBHEESHANA.)

RAMA: Vibheeshana: The dust and heat blind me – but I feel a new pulse among us. Is it He that now leads the Rakshasas to the field?

VIBHEESHANA: *(Unable to hide his pride.)* It is He, my lord – Lord of them All. The dark beating heart at the centre – is always my brother.

RAMA: *(Turning to VIBHEESHANA gently with a smile.)* You love him. More fiercely than ever.

(VIBHEESHANA looks away in shame. RAMA looks back at the advancing demon army. He watches RAVANA.)

(In a low voice to VIBHEESHANA, with great respect.)

How magnificent he truly is. If ever there was one who could have been King of the Devas…

VIBHEESHANA: But he took the way of the night, the left path of the soul and he must be stopped.

Never doubt me Rama. When the time comes, I will kill him with my own hands, if you ask.

(RAMA embraces VIBHEESHANA, who receives the strength, pulls away and nods at RAMA – who nods in return.)

VALMIKI 2: The Rakshasa King wades through the monkey men – severing limbs and torsos with terrifying ease. Sugriva heaves any rock, stone or tree he can uproot and hurl – destroying every arrow in flight. But Ravana finds his mark…

VALMIKI 1: The serpent astra buries itself in the Monkey King's breast.

(SUGRIVA falls on the blood-soaked earth.)

VALMIKI 2: Monkey arms, legs, heads lie strewn at his feet. Ravana's archery is an ancient prowess of warriors born of another age and time.

(HANUMAN, in rage at the death of his kinsmen, charges at RAVANA.)

HANUMAN: Rakshasa, you have Brahma's blessing but no protection against this monkey fist of mine.

RAVANA: Come monkey fist. Kill me if you can.

HANUMAN: Have you forgotten how I ended each of your sons yesterday?

(Enraged, RAVANA strikes at HANUMAN's chest, knocking the great Vanara to the ground. He staggers to his feet and shakes off the extraordinary force of the blow. He strikes suddenly, at the stunned demon king.)

RAVANA: *(RAVANA reels from the blow. Recovering quickly, though shaken now.)* Well done, monkey fist! More power than I thought.

VALMIKI 2: A shadow falls silently onto the battlefield now. Every Rakshasa, terrified, turns and flees.

RAVANA: From what do you dare run?

(When he looks back – it is to the awesome sight of LAKSHMANA standing UTTERLY still – watching him. They lock eyes.)

Foolish human! Prepare to pass through Yama's gates!

LAKSHMANA: I wait for you, old man. Will we talk? Or will we fight?

(RAVANA raises his bow.)

VALMIKI 1: Ravana's fiery missiles race towards Lakshmana. The kshatriya moves faster than the eye can hold. In moments, the shafts fall tamely around him – serpents without heads.

(RAVANA shouts out his admiration.)

Lakshmana sends a volley that cleaves, in two, the bow in Ravana's hand.

(RAVANA stands stunned, as blood blooms all over his awesome physique.)

VALMIKI 2: His bow in pieces, Ravana is hurt often and grievously. He invokes Brahma's feminine power and hurls it at Lakshmana. The small, deadly sun takes brother to Rama centre of the chest.

(LAKSHMANA is instantly rendered unconscious. RAVANA tries to take LAKSHMANA's body from the battlefield, but he cannot lift his weight.)

RAVANA: How is it that I, who once tore Mount Kailasa up by the roots, cannot move this human with all my strength?

HANUMAN: *(HANUMAN roars at the RAKSHASA, giving him a vicious blow. RAVANA falls, stunned.)* The man you try to raise carries Rama's Dharma. You will never carry such holy burden, Rakshasa. Who can carry such weight?

(RAVANA, bleeding from the mouth, stumbles backwards to a sitting position. HANUMAN lifts and carries LAKSHMANA to RAMA and places his silent body at RAMA's feet. RAMA falls to his knees and touches LAKSHMANA with great love.)

RAMA: When we sat as boys watching the monsoons in silence, I saw this moment once. You asked what I smiled at then. I was silent but I saw you rise from the grasp of brahmashakti. I have seen you by my side always, into the dark cave of time. Wake brother. Open your eyes.

(LAKSHMANA opens his eyes and smiles when he sees RAMA.)

VALMIKI 2: Ravana moves through the monkey-men like death. Countless vanaras fall in the wake of his fury. Their screams fill the blue Lankan skies.

(An unearthly sound rings out.)

VALMIKI 1: But a single note from Rama's bow silences all.

RAMA: Ravana, prepare for your end. Siva himself cannot offer you sanctuary from me.

VALMIKI 1: Ravana has no argument against the sea of Rama's fire.
The Blue One fights with the wisdom of the Fathers through age and time.
Ravana has no answer to the Blue One's archery.
When Ravana is on his knees like a boy, Rama prepares a final shaft –
But drops his bow…

RAMA: *(With a smile.)* Go home, Old Man.

RAVANA: *(Devastated by this humiliation, he screams.)* Lift your bow! Kill me! Anything not pity! Take my life!

RAMA: My dharma is to kill the great Ravana. Not an old man on his knees. Go home.
Return tomorrow an opponent worthy of me.

RAVANA: *(He staggers backwards.)* More savage is your "kindness" than any fire you bring.

(With profound humiliation, he leaves the battlefield.)

IV.

(SITA is in her confinement, still chanting vedas. Shafts of light suggest the setting of sun as she prays and waits. RAVANA sits on his throne – a broken version of himself. He has aged ten-fold since this all began. INDRAJIT stands before his father RAVANA. MANDODARI watches from nearby.)

INDRAJIT: To see my father, the mighty Ravana, broken like a woman… Rise and claim yourself, King of Lanka.

RAVANA: *(Almost in a trance.)* A yuga ago, I once ravished a chaste woman, Vedavati – and she cursed me. Perhaps Sita is Vedavati… Born again to be my death.

(INDRAJIT strides towards his father, yelling with disgust and rage.)

INDRAJIT: WE ARE DYING OUT THERE IN THE THOUSANDS! FOR YOU!

(RAVANA pays no attention to INDRAJIT's tirade. He turns to the silent MANDODARI.)

RAVANA: I feel I know her…from another time…

INDRAJIT: *(Desperate.)* What does Ravana want his favourite son to do?

RAVANA: *(Becoming suddenly lucid and focused.)* Bring me Rama of Ayhoda's heart by any means.

INDRAJIT: Any?

RAVANA: But do not harm Her in any way.

(INDRAJIT touches his father's feet. As he stands.)

INDRAJIT: I will fight for you, father.
But I will never forgive you for loving her more than you do me.

(He turns and leaves his father slumped in the chair hiding his face behind his hand; and his mother watching quietly from the corner.)

V.

VALMIKI 1: Hanuman leads the storming vanaras into battle. But what he sees coming is a sight none could have dreamed.

HANUMAN: STOP! Do not throw a single stone or tree.

(In INDRAJIT's arms is SITA-BODY.)

HANUMAN: Fetch Rama!

INDRAJIT: *(Grabbing her by her hair.)* Is this what you come looking for?

(Between the two armies, in front of every vanara and rakshasa – INDRAJIT grabs the SITA-BODY and kisses her violently. He strikes out and he slaps her face with such force that everyone present is stunned.)

HANUMAN: Rakshasa! You do not dare. For this you will die.

INDRAJIT: She has stolen my father's soul. I will speak for each Rakshasa life lost over this whore!

HANUMAN: Even you would not break Dharma like this, Rakshasa!

INDRAJIT: You speak of dharma, Vanara! How many women and their children perished the night you turned our city to ash? You of Rama's forces claim righteousness. But in war – it is ALWAYS the innocent who die.

(Everyone is quiet.)

(In one move, INDRAJIT snaps the SITA-BODY's neck. HANUMAN and the vanaras are stunned, motionless. None can believe what INDRAJIT has done.)

INDRAJIT: Tell Rama of Ayhoda his whore is dead.

(SITA stands in the shadows watching. She sings softly to herself.)

VI.

(RAMA stands to welcome HANUMAN as he appears, but stops short, seeing his grief.)

HANUMAN: Indrajit brought Sita to the battlefield.

(RAMA stands quietly, waiting for the fatal blow to fall on his heart.)

RAMA: And… *(Losing control.)* …SPEAK!

HANUMAN: …Broke her gentle neck.

(RAMA opens his mouth, but no sound will come. He falls to his knees. LAKSHMANA, still extremely fragile from his earlier injury, turns and grabs RAMA by the shoulders.)

LAKSHMANA: *(Filled with bitter rage.)* Stand brother! The hour is come.

(But RAMA is beyond hearing or speech.)

Brother – rise up and follow your Dharma. It is time for the Rakshasa Kinga and his son to die!

(RAMA gasps for air.)

LAKSHMANA: Will you let him defeat you in grief? Rise brother. Now is the time to honour what he has destroyed. Rama on his knees weeping – is what he was hoping for.

VIBHEESHANA: *(Without emotion.)* Where is her body?

HANUMAN: Indrajit left with it.

VIBHEESHANA: Ravana loves Sita more than his kingdom, more than his own life. He would never let Indrajit or any…

(Suddenly he understands what INDRAJIT is doing.)

O dear god! Rise! We must hurry to Nikumbhila! It was a Maya Sita that Indrajit created.

HANUMAN: *(Trying to grasp what is being said.)* A Maya Sita ?

VIBHEESHANA: A body in her likeness conjured from the mysteries of the parallel world. I have once seen him dabble such sorcery in the past. It is his cunning to shock us into grief that he may win crucial time.

HANUMAN: Time for what?

VIBHEESHANA: Indrajit is sitting yagna at this moment - to make himself invincible. If we do not stop him…All is lost!

(Turning grimly to LAKSHMANA, his face still pale – his eyes dark, he lays his hands on LAKSHMANA's bowed head. He is still unable to speak.)

LAKSHMANA: Bless me, my brother and my God. The hour of my life's purpose has come.

VII.

(INDRAJIT sits before a fire, his lean scarred body bare. He feeds the fire with ghee. Like a fierce priest, he is absorbed in his sacrifice, chanting mantras of power. VIBHEESHANA throws a stone nearby. Hearing the noise, INDRAJIT rises and comes to see who is there. Seeing his uncle, he is enraged.)

INDRAJIT: May you be damned forever for showing them our sacred Nikumbhila! We will never again speak your name in Lanka. For you betray your bretheren. And nothing is lower. *(He spits.)*

VIBHEESHANA: You may be a great warrior, child. But were you to survive the ages – you will never have the truth of the Fathers. In this, you will always be a boy.

INDRAJIT: You are a traitor. No matter what I have done – I will not have sold my own.

VIBHEESHANA: It is over, son.

INDRAJIT: *(Smiling strangely.)* Indeed. I have sat the fire and the war is now won.

VIBHEESHANA: But did you finish sitting yagna? Can you be sure?

(VIBHEESHANA sharply meets his eye. There is fear in him now.)

Or whilst you have been speaking bold words with me... Is Rama's brother not sitting comfortably at your fire. I believe the sacred blessing is now irretrievably his!

(He turns to see LAKSHMANA seated at his yagna fire. INDRAJIT freezes.)

VALMIKI 2: For the first moment in his savage life – Indrajit is afraid.

(The fight is on.)

Only the greatest archers, instructed by the most knowing gurus could match brother to Rama with Lanka's fiercest son.

VALMIKI 1: Into such battles, we meet our equal and find that we are battling our shadow:

The one that whispers to us of ourselves.

LAKSHMANA: *(In fierce prayer, drawing the bow.)* If the Ishvaku Line have always honoured their word – let this moment be Indrajit's last.

(He launches an arrow. When the blinding light of the astra fades, LAKSHMANA stands covered in INDRAJIT's blood. Of INDRAJIT's body nothing remains.)

VIII.

(RAVANA is on his knees, roaring at the news of the death of his son. MANDODARI stands, fist over mouth, nearby. RAVANA rises like a tidal wave and moves to the cell where SITA is kept. She is standing as he enters, ready for him – fire raging in her eyes.)

RAVANA: My sons are dead and Lanka lies in ruins.

(SITA matches his stare.)

SITA: You can kill me – but you will not have me.
You can take me but I will not be yours.
In this life time and all those to come – I will never love you.
Take my life, Rakshasa!
I am ready – to die.

RAVANA: It is not your life I come for.

(He is moving towards her with resolve and intent.)

I hear your wings beating against the broken window of my hatred. We will drown together, Daughter of Janaka. Like you – I am not afraid to die.

SITA: What will this profit you? The battle is lost.

RAVANA: Your Rama has one fatal flaw. He is a man. And though he will despise himself for it – he will never want you again. For I know best of all: The battle of the self is the hardest won of any war.

SITA: You give up everything for this?

RAVANA: Our destinies will die together, Child of the Dharma.

(He moves to the SITA-BODY. He tears the clothes from it and rapes it with pure violence. SITA stands at some distance, quietly watching as

the SITA-BODY takes the force. He looks up to find SITA staring deeply into his eyes.)

Don't look at me!

(Roaring.) LOOK AWAY!

(But she stares at him unflinchingly – for the duration of the rape.)

(RAVANANA stands. He looks now only at the SITA-BODY curled in a foetal position on the floor. He backs out and away.)

VALMIKI 1: Essence and Body wait – like sisters – to float back in to one another after the storm.

(MANDODARI steps out of the shadows. She gathers the broken and bleeding SITA-BODY into her arms. They are both weeping. MANDODARI begins to sing her an ancient lullaby. SITA watches from nearby. She sings too.)

MANDODARI: History has been kind to me. Called me faithful and true. But when I saw what kind of devotion he was capable of after all...

(RAVANA walks onto the battlefield alone. His arms open wide, he shows he is unarmed. The boys KUSA and LAVA sing in their haunting pitch as RAMA approaches. LAKSHMANA has a weapon poised and HANUMAN stands some distance away – ready for an attack from the Lord of the Rakshasas. RAVANA looks deeply into RAMA's eyes.)

RAMA: What makes you weep, Rakshasa? What makes you smile?

RAVANA: My sons are dead, my city in ashes, my harem empty, my legions slain.
I kneel before you – as naked as a newborn.

RAMA: On broken knees... but I smell no shame.

RAVANA: *(Shrugging.)* This war has been fought in ages gone. It will be fought again and again. Our story will never end.

RAMA: I will find you as the tide rises in every age. We will face each other always with you on broken knees.

RAVANA: And you will lose her in every lifetime – as you do today.

RAMA: Sita lives.

RAVANA: In me and I in her.

(RAMA stands back startled, though he retains his poise of certainty.)

I am sated finally. I believe she feels the same.

(RAMA stands perfectly still for several long moments, searching for the truth in RAVANA's eyes. RAMA lifts his sword, his hand shaking with tension about to be released by his rage. But he stops to see a woman enter the battlefield. It is MANDODARI. She comes to her husband who is moments from death.)

RAVANA: *(Not taking his eyes from RAMA, he tells MANDODARI.)* Go home.

MANDODARI: I will speak.

RAVANA: *(Ferociously.)* WOMAN! GO HOME!

RAMA: *(Sensing the power of her intention.)* Speak…

MANDODARI: *(To RAVANA.)* Love of my life: I have a tale to tell. And it will be the last thing you live to hear: A tale designed a thousand leagues below an ocean – dark through the ages – where nothing will ever shine. I take it upon my shoulders. A stone that will bring me no peace but, at last, makes my suffering real. Mine is a tale of she whose name was Mandodari in this life. A great queen. Her husband tore her from her mother when she was still a child, and shaped her to his desires… Grew her to his tastes – like a plant turned downwards from the sun. Her husband was a great Rakshasa. Perhaps the greatest ever lived. He held the three realms: Swarga, Bhumi and Patala with ease in a single hand. Yet Mandodari's life was a desert of nothing but desire and shame. Not a night passed that she did not lay hungering for her king. Hating yet hungering – she slowly drew away from the light until she knew nothing outside of him alone. He came for her less and less as his harem grew. She thought perhaps some day he would be satiated with the endless new bodies open to him. But as he consumed – so his hunger over the years – grew. Yearning for the urgency of his battle-scarred body, time passed as a daily eternity, yet spilled extravagantly through her fingers as years. Her leaves turned gold and then grey and floated away.

RAVANA: I never stopped…

MANDODARI: *(Raising a hand to silence him.)* One night she woke alone again. As she lay watching the moonlight shift across the walls of her cell, she knew that at last she hated him more than she needed him to come for her. She wanted suddenly to see him suffer as she had all these years. And there came a day when she knew she had the means. For, though she had told nobody – Mandodari was with child. And she was certain that growing in her was, at last, a girl: The daughter that Ravana had longed for more than anything else. Here, finally, was something she could take instead of give. And she sang to the pain and joy growing in her womb. She hid the swelling planes of her body from all – merely sent a message to her husband that she wished to go on pilgrimage to the Holy Trithas. He agreed, though he did not come and say goodbye. Perhaps that was the last possibility that their fates could have shifted. But he stayed away. She hardened her heart for what lay ahead.

(RAVANA turns from where he is kneeling, to stare at MANDODARI – struck dumb by what she is unravelling before him.)

Mandodari knew the child in her womb was no ordinary life. The wife of Ravana knew peace in those months for the first time in her life. Away from Lanka, her body growing heavier each day – she carried a peace borne of the promise of coming revenge. And for once – the burning was still. In her ninth month, she mounted a stallion and rode dazed and utterly alone through the world until she felt the first savage tug in her womb. She drifted between sleep and wakefulness on the forest's edge. For hours, she lay in her body of sorrow and wept for the child she would never know. At dawn, she rose and managed a few steps toward the nearby city, before her birth waters broke. Squatting down in a field alone, she pushed life from her and held in her arms a golden baby girl. Never had she known what she felt as she held the child for that short hour. Her daughter's eyes watching up at her with their ancient questions, the small mouth waiting for her mother's breast. But vengeance was the only thing that would make life in Lanka bearable for Mandodari in her remaining years. With a last kiss – she laid the child down on the earth, buried her birth sack and umbilical chord close by, climbed her black steed and rode back to Lanka alone. As dawn broke – it is told – Janaka of Mathila moved through the morning light, towards a field on the southern outskirts of his land. With his golden plough, he wanted to turn the earth for a sacrifice that morning.

(RAVANA begins to moan like a beast.)

And there in a furrow of the earth he found a baby girl.

RAVANA: NO…No please no…

MANDODARI: He named her Sita. Took her home and raised her as his own. That body you have loved, used, broken. She is your only daughter. Your own flesh, blood and bone.

(RAVANA screams like a wild beast. He turns on all fours – clawing at his face. He is unable to bear the pain of being in his own body. RAMA stands like a stone. RAVANA's screams bellow through the city of Lanka.)

RAMA: Janaki. Janaki….

RAVANA: *(Pleading.)* Do it. Please. I beg you. End me.

(RAMA plunges the weapon into the Rakshasa's heart. All turn to MANDODARI who is standing as though already absent, lost in the void of her own terrible design.)

MANDODARI: *(To all of us who witness her, but really to herself.)* Do you know what it is to be born woman into this realm? To be used and shaped before your soul or body are formed. To be had and discarded? Torn and broken. Waiting, waiting for reasons to make themselves plain. Until you understand there is no reason. Just plans we can grow in the dark. And wait for the day to take back what was stolen from us as girls.

LAKSHMANA: Your so you sacrificed your own daughter?

MANDODARI: I thought she was safe because of the curse: If he ravaged a woman – he would die.

RAMA: *(In a whisper.)* Did he touch her?

MANDODARI: *(Weeping.)* I did not count on Ravana being willing to lose everything for a woman To give his life.

RAMA: DID HE TOUCH HER?

MANDODARI: When I saw the devotion he was capable of for a woman, after all…I left him to the fate he fashioned for himself.

RAMA: *(Weeping.)* Sita?

MANDODARI: *(Weeping too.)* I lost my way…Called her name. But once entered – there was no way back. *(She is silent.)* Take my life. It is yours.

RAMA: *(Shaking his head – broken.)* Take it yourself. From me you will get nothing more.

MANDODARI: *(She turns from him to walk away.)* We find it easy to pin the darkness of the world's story on a woman's breast. But I was made in Ravana's heart. Fired in his kiln. The product of his male soul. While they fight out their ownership of us on battlefields, can they ever know the suffering we must endure? We become what shapes us. We learn to survive alone.

(To RAMA.) Tell Sita that I love her; loved her the day I laid her in the earth that morning; love her still. I chose the left hand way – for though I loved her…I hated her father more.

(She turns and walks out into the wilderness. RAMA is on his knees.)

6. Home

I.

(HANUMAN is kneeling before SITA-BODY who stands. Her face is bruised, streaked with dirt and tears. Her eyes are calm but she trembles from the violence still. SITA watches her body gently from a distance.)

SITA-BODY: *(In a whisper.)* Hanuman, Lord of Devotion. *(He lays himself at her feet.)*

HANUMAN: Gracious one, Ravana is dead,

(SITA-BODY kneels and kisses the ground. When she tries to rise, she stumbles. HANUMAN moves to help.)

SITA-BODY: I will do it alone.

(Which she does, with great pain and dignity.)

Has my Rama come for me?

HANUMAN: He waits outside.

(Her eyes fill with tears of joy.)

SITA-BODY: Tell him I am here when he is ready.

HANUMAN: He asked that we first bring you this holy water for the women to bathe you in and these finest silks in which you are to be dressed.

SITA-BODY: *(She looks at him for a long moment.)* I need no silk or waters, Hanuman.

HANUMAN: He said to tell you: He cannot bear to see you in your suffering. He wishes you the time to gather your Self, and return to him as you once were.

SITA-BODY: *(To herself, grappling.)* As she once was…

(She looks over her shoulder at SITA who stands watching her. SITA-BODY is quiet. HANUMAN hands the fabric and perfumes to the women. As they move towards SITA, she raises her hand.)

Tell Rama I will meet him as I am.

(He nods, understanding her courage. He bows deeply, and turns to go.)

Hanuman…

(He turns back to her.)

Your devotion. Your heart…They go with me always.

(HANUMAN raises his hands together in humility to his forehead in thanks.)

HANUMAN: As long as you are remembered, Devi – I will walk this world.

(He bows deeply again and then leaves her.)

SITA: *(To the women.)* Take those fabrics and perfumes for new brides at their beginning. Tell my Rama I am ready to be seen. As I am.

(The women around her bow and leave her. Alone, she looks over her shoulder at SITA, who nods, smiles gently and with great love. She is ready to go out.)

II.

(Outside, RAMA is anxious.)

(LAKSHMANA, VIBHEESHANA, SUGRIVA and HANUMAN look at one another, unsure of RAMA's intention. They wait with unease. Finally SITA-BODY appears and walks towards RAMA. Despite her ravaged state, she is incandescent. RAMA's eyes fill with tears. All internal conflict falling away, he looks at her with profound love.)

RAMA: *(Whispers.)* My Love.

SITA-BODY: My Lord.

(They stand looking at one another in silence. The VALMIKIS sing softly of love. SITA BODY reaches to wipe RAMA's tears. But with titanic effort, he holds his hand up and turns his face away. SITA-BODY is stunned.)

Rama?

RAMA: *(In a whisper.)* Sita. But no longer mine. *(SITA-BODY exhales as though struck.)*

SITA: *(Standing at a distance, watching.)* This body…

RAMA: Once touched…can never be untouched again.

SITA: …Was made only for sorrow.

SITA-BODY: *(Gathering herself, she is trembling, but centred now.)* My Lord.
Your Wife stands before you.
Honour her.
She has travelled a great distance over time.

RAMA: *(His face twisted with conflict.)* What man takes home his
wife, fresh from Ravana of Lanka's bed?

SITA-BODY: What man speaks such words to me?

RAMA: Rama of Ayhoda speaks.

SITA-BODY: *(Shaking her head.)* No. The ego shadow is a fine
sand that blows into the finest cracks. But not the heart of my
Rama. For there is no space in there – not occupied by love.

RAMA: Do you know who you are, Sita of Lanka?

SITA-BODY: *(Looking him directly in the eyes.)* I, my Lord, am Sita
of Time.
Daughter to The Great Mother.
Reeling back in over circles of pain.

RAMA: It has been said…

SITA-BODY: *(Interrupting him firmly but gently.)* I care nothing for
what is said. Only for what is.

RAMA: *(With despair.)* Who are you?

SITA: In this life I am called Sita. Wife to you in all.

RAMA: Did he touch you? Your father…

SITA-BODY: *(Tenderly, with hand on her heart.)* Only you touch me.

RAMA: *(Losing control.)* DID HE TOUCH YOU?

SITA: *(Steadfast.)* Only you.

RAMA: *(Unable to look at her or to look away.)* Your body is now
his…

SITA-BODY: This body?
This body is not his to take.

Nor yours to have.
Or mine to give.
I have loaned it from the Great Mother. Like everything, she will soon take it back. But who I am – the flame that burns within this clay – is mine to offer. And that light has been yours since the day we first met at the river, both barely 16 summers grown.

(RAMA shakes his head, eyes closed, in deepest battle with himself. His voice trembles with emotion.)

RAMA: The body is sacred...

SITA-BODY: Body, my love, is subject to the wind: The manifestation of all we have lived. There is that which we choose for it – and that which others will write on our skin. But in matters of the soul – our choices are always our own. And I chose You. Even as you show me your shadow now – I choose you again.

(She reaches for his hand, but he cannot respond. She speaks softly.)

Come with me, beloved, back into the dark forest of our love.
Forward into the blinding light of tomorrow.
Come with me, to a place beyond this body I must wear.
Let's walk beside one another along the narrow, overgrown path –
Back, back to when we are no longer afraid.

(The VALMIKIS sing softly of love.)

RAMA: *(RAMA turns from her.)* I swore to rescue you.
I owe you nothing more.

SITA-BODY: You who has known me better than I know myself,
You who has touched the dark waters of my soul

RAMA: *(With resolve.)* Build a fire. Walk the flames of truth and prove your purity for everyone here.

SITA-BODY: Am I not standing in the centre of your fire right now?
It is more intense than anything you could manifest from wood.
I burn with questions you would have no answers for.

Questions that would make Ash of your small, frightened words.

But here is my love evident: I do not turn away.
I see your fear and I sing to you across the shifting, barren desert sands:
Beloved, do not be afraid.
Come with me, where nothing binds us to the womb of this small world.
Come with me to the edge of the forest to slip away in the dark.
Let's chase the lengthening shadows to the end of Danaka Vana and lie in her arms.

(RAMA covers his face. SITA looks on with great love. He looks up – gentle and broken now.)

RAMA: Janaki, Janaki… My duty – before being a husband – is to be King. We cannot choose our Dharma. My people must come first. And they will always question your purity. How can I lead them when they doubt the very foundations of my own home?

SITA-BODY: Dance them through this shadow, Rama. They are frightened children who need you to light the way. Their fear for a woman's chastity is merely an infant's longing to have the Great Mother all to one's self. My "purity" lost is death your people fear. Yoni – the sacred Feminine Passage – brought us each life. But it threatens with proximity to the darkness from which we each barely emerged. Help your people to remember what it is, to love beyond ideas.

RAMA: Did he have you Janaki? I must know.
Did you surrender to Ravana's power?

SITA-BODY: Let only women speak of "surrender" for now. We bear children in the grip of death; we are humbled monthly by pain. Many of us have been forced flat and destroyed by another's violence – torn into against what we choose. Those who have endured this – know that it is possible to die… though the body lives on. To accuse us "surrender" having survived this violation, is to fail us at love's most sacred core.

And when we are doubted by the very He whose name was the single mantra we uttered again and again just to survive... This a pain more profound than the profanation of one's own womb. Stand beside me and let me find that not my body – but the Turning Divinity in me – is my true worth in your eyes.

(RAMA is weeping softly.)

(She whispers.) Come with me, my love, back to where the forest grew around us like arms in love's dark, strong embrace. Come with me to where the light of tomorrow shines and life flourishes despite the fear and the pain.

(RAMA covers his face.)

RAMA: Forgive me, my love. Forgive me. I am only a man.

SITA-BODY: In this messy struggle with the soul – not your godly perfection, but simply Rama the Man – can talk to us from the pain of being mortal and small. It is the imperfect Rama who will finally lead us home.

RAMA: *(Gathering her towards him.)* He hurt you, my love...

SITA-BODY: Yes. But I am here.
And if I am Ravana's daughter... In the darkness of his longing – he ravaged only himself. Weep for Ravana of Lanka. He is all of us in the vortex of hunger. He is innocence who forgot that, in this life – we all answer to the same family name.

RAMA: *(Kneeling before her.)* Keeper of the Dharma. Mother to us all.

(She takes his face in her hands and looks into his eyes.)

SITA-BODY: Rama, take me home.

(KUSA and LAVA sing out as RAMA and SITA dissolve into dark.)

III.

(The shape of their bodies form again in white light, moving as though on horseback, through the lands they left. RAMA sits behind SITA-BODY, holding her close as KUSA and LAVA sing. LAKSHMANA, VIBHEESHANA, HANUMAN, SUGRIVA ride nearby. SITA watches them go.)

VALMIKI 1: Ayhoda, like Lanka, has nine city gates. Nine entry points to the heart. And we can only know the joy of coming home for the painful blessing of having left at all.

RAMA: *(Standing where he once stood to say goodbye to his birth-land.)* Land of my ancestors, Gods of Kosala: Thanks be for this day of our return.

(He kisses the Earth. SITA-BODY does the same behind him – as does the rest of the traveling party. KAUSALYA, whose hair is now entirely white, walks towards and embraces them. She is frail, but as present as ever.)

SITA: What lands we had wandered to in the shadows of our souls. The ocean's salt tide in us, pulled back to Ayhoda. At last the time of Ramaraja was here. You gave Ayhoda the heartbeat it had longed for. Some say those days lasted eleven thousand years. Never had any leader the devotion of the people like you, beloved.

(SITA watches from the shadows as RAMA lies over the SITA-BODY.)

KAUSALYA: Yoni-Lingam – the sacred union: Perfect in the struggle and imperfection. Lingam pushes forward into the dark archway. And into life it is borne. The going into is where we find entry to the fires of this world.

SITA: And the night came to pass when I dreamed of twin boys singing to me from my womb.

(RAMA lies beside SITA-BODY and runs his hand over her large pregnant belly.)

Our sons had emerged from the dense static of the In – Between;
Into the gateway of that first single heart beat They were, at last, safely in my body of this world.

(The Street Boys continue their desolate, beautiful song.)

IV.

(RAMA is seated in a circle, in counsel with KAUSALYA, LAKSHMANA and VIBHEESHANA. SITA-BODY remains in repose at the centre, asleep. Her huge belly is the manifest reason they are gathered. In reality, she lies in another room.)

RAMA: Sita's time draws near.

KAUSALYA: We count the days that her tide brings your sons, as we *(smiling.)* of failing eyes and yellowed teeth – prepare to slip back into the waters that once brought us to these shores.

RAMA: *(He nods to his mother and looks around at the trusted faces.)* My sacred circle who guard and protect me – heart, body, soul...
I have heard whisperings and want to know if what I fear is true: Tell me what my people say of Sita and the new lives she carries now.

(There is a deep silence of sudden unease. SITA-BODY sighs quietly and repositions her sleeping form. RAMA looks at his consorts – waiting, yet knowing that he will hear what he fears most.)

Vibheeshana? Brother of Lanka once – but now to us all: What is it my subjects whisper when they see my Sita pass, heavy with salt waters and new life?

(VIBHEESHANA is silent, looking at his hands, trembling with emotion as RAMA watches him and waits.)

VIBHEESHANA: *(Quietly.)* They speak of how Rama is just and fair and true. They pray every morning and evening that the reign of Rama never end for us all.

RAMA: *(After a long pause.)* Lakshmana? Brother to my blood...

LAKSHMANA: *(He, too, is struggling.)* They speak of your impeccable Dharma; How you made your bow sing across the battlefield before you felled Ravana of Darkness; How in courage – you have no equal. Never will.

(RAMA is silent. Finally he turns to KAUSALYA.)

RAMA: Mother – perhaps only a woman will have the courage to tell me what my people say?

(KAUSALYA and all the women – SITA-BODY, SITA, VALMIKIS – all deeply inhale.)

KAUSALYA: *(She turns and looks RAMA deep in the eyes. And though hers fill with tears, she never looks away.)* They say that your Sita is a stain on the Ishvaku name.

(The room is thick with silence. KAUSALYA continues. She speaks now without pause.)

They say that which is touched can never be untouched again. They say that if their King accepts a woman who has known the weight of another man, then what is to stop their wives from laying down where they may grow dark with flies. They say the twin boys Sita carries are the children of Ravana of Lanka. Others whisper that the unborn boys lie in her womb, hand in hand: One… the son of Rama Blue Prince of Grace. The other… the spawn of the Rakshasa's loins. And that we will never know which babe comes in darkness, until it's too late. They whisper that for you they would walk the earth over jagged glass – but that Sita should be taken with her unborn sons, so deep into Danaka Vana – that she never find her way to Ayhoda again. She is loved fiercely by the People. They need her. They weep to see her. They kiss her hands and take the dust from her feet. They know the depth of what she is. But they wait, like wolves when the scent is on the wind, to see her destroyed.

(KAUSALYA and all the women – SITA-BODY, SITA, VALMIKIS – all exhale deeply.)

That, my son, is the truth I offer from my bones.

RAMA: *(Looking directly at KAUSALYA.)* Thank you, ma.

(RAMA rises and walks away to stand alone. He covers his head and face with his hands. He speaks softly with himself – the despair and grief soaking through the whispered words. He is praying for strength. The others wait in respectful silence where he has left them. All of them keep their eyes cast down. SITA walks to RAMA gently and kisses his forehead – though he cannot see her. SITA-BODY murmurs in her sleep. The VALMIKIS begin a low note of chanting. RAMA gathers himself and returns to where the others wait.)

(With numbed detachment.)

Sita wishes to visit a great rishi's asrama for his blessing tomorrow and plans to spend the night. In the morning, Lakshmana, you will cross the Ganga and ride beyond the frontiers of Kosala. You will bring Sita to the banks of Tamasa – as she expects. But *(Almost breathless.)* she will never return to Ayhoda in this lifetime again. You will leave her and her unborn sons alone there.

(LAKSHMANA and VIBHEESHANA gasp. KAUSALYA is silent, breathlessly watching her son.)

LAKSHMANA: This! Because the people talk?

RAMA: I am here to serve. Without the people's faith, I cannot lead. Though they love her, they doubt her purity still…

(They are silent. LAKSHMANA looks up at RAMA finally – with steel in his eyes.)

LAKSHMANA: Abandon Sita on the shores of the wild, pregnant and alone?

This, Rama, you will have to do for yourself!

(RAMA looks at LAKSHMANA. They stare deeply at one another. It is a look of bitter challenge from LAKSHMANA that has never been there before.)

VIBHEESHANA: *(Gently, trying reason.)* Lord Rama, the people will never understand a chastity like Sita's. Teach them. They long for you to show the way.

RAMA: *(Without having taken his eyes from LAKSHMANA's, he speaks with grim resolve.)* Brothers, you will do as I have said, or you may no longer call Ayhoda home.

(With emotion straining to break through.)

Tell her I was called away urgently.
I cannot say goodbye. My strength will fail me.
Now go!

(LAKSHMANA backs out of the room, longing for RAMA to change what he has ordered him to do. They all leave – except KAUSALYA who

remains. She walks around him to face him. He looks at her – his face now contorted with conflict and pain. She takes his face in her hands and stares deeply into his eyes.)

KAUSALYA: Do you know who you are, son?

RAMA: Who am I, mother? Who am I? King. But only a man. Yet I am called to sacrifice what I value most.

(RAMA falls to his knees, praying for strength. KAUSALYA holds his head against her belly as he weeps like a child. All the women begin to hum.)

KAUSALYA: Will there ever come a time when we understand just how much fear, how much hatred is inspired by our form. From us they emerge. Into us – they penetrate. At us they hurl their stones and hate. And in us curl like a child when once again alone. Shadow lives like its own pregnancy – ever waiting to have us borne back into the dark eye of the storm.

(She holds him a moment longer and then walks away, leaving him broken and sobbing on his knees on the floor.)

V.

(LAKSHMANA rows, watching SITA-BODY, who is facing the water at the small boat's helm. She is radiant with joy. When they are midstream, SITA-BODY folds her hands and prays to the Ganga. When she is finished, she looks out onto the waters with a hand on her belly.)

SITA-BODY: Ganga – whom the Devis bathed in…

(She looks behind her when she hears LAKSHMANA's trembling breath.)

Lakshmana?

LAKSHMANA: I was just remembering when we last crossed her…

SITA-BODY: But this time we know we will return home.

(When they reach land, LAKSHMANA, despite himself, buckles over with the pain.)

SITA-BODY: Brother, what is it?

(She watches him for a moment and then her spine straightens.)

(She nods, turns and walks away. He goes after her. He catches her as she falls.)

SITA-BODY: *(Crying out with her whole soul.)* This body was made only for sorrow.

(LAKSHMANA can only weep. Slowly she gathers herself and pulls away.)

Tell them not to grieve for me, brother. For I am now gone.
I will never return in this life again.
Go now while you have strength.

(He walks around her in pradakshina, weeping silently. He lays at her feet and she blesses him.)

Dear Lakshmana…You who has watched over me always:
May you forgive yourself and find peace again someday.

(He stands and looks her in the eyes. Then he turns and steps into the boat. She watches as it leaves the shore, and then the shadows fall around and over her as she disappears into the dark.)

(A shadow of the great eagle JATAVU moves overhead. The plastic covers on the scaffolding tremor and KUSA and LAVA begin to sing.)

VI.

(SITA-BODY lies dead, face down – arms stretched wide in the earth's embrace. KAUSALYA and MANDODARI as VALMIKI SAMAJ stand beside the corpse.)

VALMIKI 1: No one knows how she survived alone on those shores. She held on until her due time came to push her twin boys into the world.

(LAKSHMANA's boat is passing through the dark water. His face is buried in his hands. He looks up.)

LAKSHMANA: Who's there?

(A boat like his own moves through the waters in the direction from where he came. He stares through the mist and dark, trying to make out who stands, watching the water beneath their boat.)

Who passes these waters in silence when a friend calls out?

(LAKSHMANA raises his bow and takes aim.)

Answer me or I must take you as my enemy. Speak now.

(The figure answers back quietly. It is the voice of RAMA – though the person shadowed.)

RAMA-FIGURE: When we watched the rain fall as small boys in our secret cave, I used to weep. And you sat beside me in silence and faith with a piece of bread, ready to serve me when my hunger woke. Brother – do not look for Rama. He is now gone. His Dharma was to serve his people. And the only way to lead is to show them what they have lost.

SITA: *(Smiling at RAMA gently and reaching over SITA-BODY and the waters.)* Come with me, beloved, back into the dark forest of our love.
Forward into the blinding light of tomorrow's promise.
Come. Let us run through time.
Like children, when once we were not afraid.

VALMIKI 2: *(Standing with the other sanitation women around the SITA-BODY.)* We found her in death – just as Janaka had found her at dawn in a furrow of the earth, when she herself was borne. Lying in the dark arms of her Mother – at last she had been gathered her home.

(VIBHEESHANA is at RAMA's side, trying to wake him. He is naked, lying in a fetal position.)

VIBHEESHANA: My Lord? My Lord? Wake up. The light has long come and gone.

(He listens at his chest and then sits up – a cry of mourning erupting from him.)

RAMA-FIGURE: *(To LAKSHMANA who continues to listen on the dark waters.)*
Until the queen, the base, the great holder of the sacred passage and heart, keeper of the Dharma, mother to us all…is welcome – Rama-Sita cannot call this Home.

SITA: *(Stretching out her arms from the shore over the dead SITA-BODY.)*
Come with me, my Love, where nothing binds us to the womb of this small world.

Come with me to the edge of the forest's warm nights…to slip away and be wild hearts again, in the fires of everything we hold.

(KAUSALYA is at VIBHEESHANA's side now, looking at the empty body of RAMA, lying curled up on the floor. She loosens her long white hair, removes her shoes and sits on the floor beside her son. She pulls his dead body into her embrace.)

KAUSALYA: *(As though she now understands.)* Only a man, my son. But True King after all.
You were leaving us – never her.
I understand now why you wept, my only boy.

VALMIKI 2: Lying in the arms of the Mother – the flies already breaking down what we believe is forever ours. But always She will have the final word.

(The women are gathered around the SITA-BODY. They turn her over and find two newborn boys. The women lift the babies.)

At her breasts…Lava and Kusa – a few hours. Old.

(They move slowly away to her left and right. The umbilical chords remain attached getting longer and longer, with the SITA-BODY still connected to them: A ragged goddess wired to these two new babies. The STREET BOYS sing their wild and urgent song of the vedas, calling us on the street. Urban rhythms grow with the sound.)

We took them in and taught them the song of their birthright – to be sung as long as there are men and women in the world.

LAKSHMANA: *(To the figure in the shadows of the boat beside his.)* But who will lead us if you are gone?

RAMA-FIGURE: My rightful heirs.

VALMIKI 2: On every corner we pass – they call to us still.

RAMA – FIGURE: There is no Ayhoda but the heart of the people. On the street, they will carry the word…

VALMIKI 1: Our unclaimed children who travel the ages, to call us up from our slumber; To cast off numbness; To remember all we have lost.

LAKSHMANA: Who speaks to me, if Rama is gone?

RAMA-FIGURE: I came – as Matsya, Kurma, Varaha, Narasimha, Vamana and Parasurama – every age to manifest dharma. Incarnated as a kshatriya this time, but always, Lord Vishnu himself: Come again from age to age to protect and repair our world. He who brings this message is Yama Deva – Death himself.

(SITA opens her arms as RAMA's boat reaches her shores. They fold into each other's powerful embrace.)

KAUSALYA: It is she who holds him at the base of his power. The surrendering that tears down all arguments against the thrusting sea. The capacity to hold and hold him – while he battles the coming storms.

VALMIKI 1: But who among us will recognize ourselves, when finally, all the mathematics of time contrive to have us pass by the very street corner, just as our story is sung? To fall to our knees in recognition. To grieve and finally die into life.

(KUSA and LAVA sing full voiced as the WOMEN lift the SITA-BODY. They make supplications to the SITA-BODY organs – asking them to return to their sources. They are chanting.)

Vision returns to the Sun.
Mind to the Moon
Body to the ground.
And Prana – Breath of Life – to the cosmic eternal that is without end.

(The SITA-BODY exhales a thin stream of mist. The plastic sheets covering the scaffolding and walls are released and float to the ground.)

(The vedic chants assume an increasing contemporary urban rythm – as the stage fills with the company dressed in modern urban gear – all attached to ipods, chords and one another – passing around KUSA and LAVA singing – who stand in downtown urban chaos, plastic bags swirling around their feet.)

Epilogue

(SITA and RAMA watch from the periphery, hand in hand.)

SITA: Do not grieve for us, beloveds. For we are now gone. Freer
than you are, still in the body of pain.
Made only for sorrow.
But from sorrow we have much to learn.
Burn after reading it – but read it well.
The beauty, the loss, the grieving.
There on the skin, in those bones, beneath those feet you have
worn for this life.
On every street corner – Ayhoda calls.

(Turning into the darkness with RAMA, she looks back one last time.)

We wait in the moving Danaka Vana.
Look for us.
We are there.

(SITA-RAMA slips away into black.)

*(The Vedas, sung by the STREET BOYS fill the space, throbbing with
urgency, as lights fade. Only the cyclorama glows – filled with a static
snow pattern once again.*

*HANUMAN – in a single shaft of light – reaches out to catch something
soft that floats down into his open palm. Blackout.)*

ENDS